Collins Primary Maths
Pupil Book 3

Series Editor: Peter Clarke

Authors: Andrew Edmondson, Elizabeth Jurgensen,
Jeanette Mumford, Sandra Roberts

Contents

	To calculate the range of a set of data	
Shape and space: (reflective symmetry, reflection and translation)/Reasoning and generalising about shapes	To recognise reflective symmetry in regular polygons: for example, know that a square has four axes of symmetry and an equilateral triangle has three	66–67
	To complete symmetrical patterns with two lines of symmetry at right angles (using squared paper or pegboard)	68–69
	To recognise where a shape will be after reflection in a mirror line parallel to one side (sides not all parallel or perpendicular to the mirror line)	70–71, 72–73 74–75, 76–77
	To make and investigate a general statement about familiar shapes by finding examples that satisfy it	78–79, 80–81
	To recognise where a shape will be after a Translation	
Measures: (time)/Problems involving measures (time)/Making decisions	To use all four operations to solve simple word problems involving numbers and quantities based on measures (time), using one or more steps	82–83, 84–85
	To use timetables	
Measures: (capacity)/Problems involving measures (capacity)/Making decisions	To convert larger to smaller units	86–87
	To choose and use appropriate number operations to solve problems, and appropriate ways of calculating: mental, mental with jottings, written methods, calculator	
	To record estimates and readings from scales to a suitable degree of accuracy	88–89, 90–91
	To use, read and write standard metric units of capacity (l, ml), including their abbreviations and relationships between them	92–93
	To know imperial units (pint, gallon)	94–95
Mental calculation strategies (+ and −)	To use known facts and place value for mental addition and subtraction: add or subtract any pair of two-digit numbers, including crossing the hundreds boundary; add several numbers	96–97
Rapid recall of addition and subtraction facts/Mental calculation strategies (+ and −)	To derive quickly or continue to derive quickly all two-digit pairs that total 100; decimals that total 1 or 10	98–99, 102–103
	To use known number facts and place value for mental addition and subtraction	
Rapid recall of addition facts/Pencil and paper procedures (+)	To extend written methods to: column addition of two integers less than 10 000; addition of a pair of decimal fractions, both with one or both with two decimal places	100–101
Properties of numbers and number sequences	To find all pairs of factors of any number up to 100	106–107, 108–109 110–111
	To make general statements about odd or even numbers, including outcome of sums and differences	
Reasoning and generalising about numbers or shapes	To explain a generalised relationship (formula) in words	112–113 114–115

Grids

Practice

1 Copy and complete the multiplication and division grids.

a

×	10	100
4		
38		
92		
61		

b

÷	10	100
6400		
1700		
280		
320		

c

×	100	10
74		
99		
18		
461		

d

÷	100	10
500		
1020		
750		
920		

e

×	10	100
42		
28		
380		
56		

2 Read these numbers. In each number one digit is red.
What does that digit represent?

a 405 395

b 123 307

c 265 788

d 350 211

e 896 473

f 157 699

g 352 147

h 452 361

i 900 254

j 871 320

3 Now add 1 to all the numbers in question 2.

Refresher

Covering counters

Play this game with a partner. You both need about 10 counters of your colour.

1　Take it in turns to choose one of these operations and one of the numbers.

×10, ×100, ÷10, ÷100　　600, 3, 80, 1000, 4600, 5000, 900, 7, 120, 40

2　Multiply or divide them to make one of the numbers on the board.

3　If you are right, cover the number with one of your counters.

4　The winner is the first person to get four counters in a line in any direction.

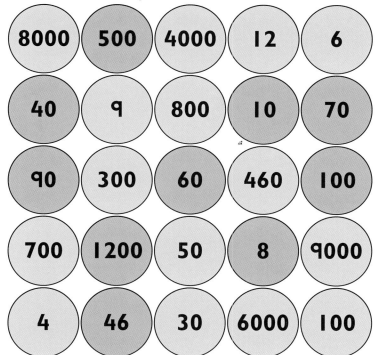

8000	500	4000	12	6
40	9	800	10	70
90	300	60	460	100
700	1200	50	8	9000
4	46	30	6000	100

Challenge

Use multiplying and dividing by 10 and 100 to answer these questions.

1　What is one tenth of:

　a　600　　　　b　2000　　　　c　180　　　　d　3400　　　　e　2500

2　What is one hundredth of:

　a　9000　　　　b　300　　　　c　3900　　　　d　3700　　　　e　520

● Use the vocabulary of estimation and approximation
● Make and justify estimates of large numbers, and estimate simple proportions such as one third, seven tenths
● Develop calculator skills and use a calculator effectively

Estimating

Practice

1 Estimate the position of each arrow on the three number lines.

a

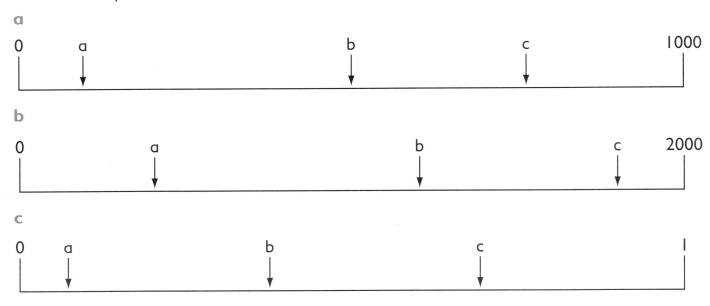

2 Work out these estimates. Explain how you worked them out.

a Estimate how many apples you eat – first in a week,
then in a year.

b Estimate how many phone calls you make in a week – first in a week,
then in a year.

c Estimate how many pencils there are in the school.

d Estimate how many 1p coins will make a straight line
1 metre long.

e Estimate how many petals in a bunch of large daisies.

Use a calculator to help you.

Refresher

1 These jars hold 100 sweets when they are full. Estimate how many are left in each jar.

a    b    c    d

2 These bottles hold 1 litre of water when full. Estimate how much water is left in each bottle.

a    b    c    d

3 Estimate the position of each arrow on the number lines.

a

```
0        a              b        c          100
|        ↓              ↓        ↓           |
```

b

```
0          a      b                    c      200
|          ↓      ↓                    ↓       |
```

c

```
0   a       b                       c        500
|   ↓       ↓                       ↓         |
```

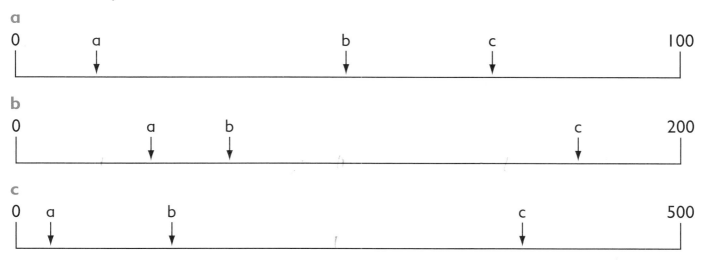

Challenge

Estimate how many breaths you take in a week.

Crossing zero

Practice

Look at each thermometer and answer the question.

a If the thermometer drops by 6° what will the temperature be?

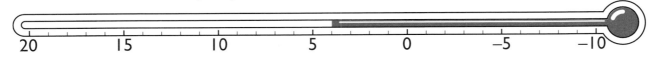

b If the thermometer drops by 5° what will the temperature be?

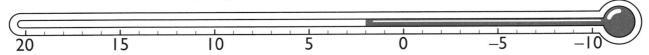

c If the thermometer rises by 6° what will the temperature be?

d If the thermometer drops by 10° what will the temperature be?

e If the thermometer rises by 12° what will the temperature be?

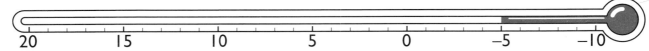

f If the thermometer rises by 9° what will the temperature be?

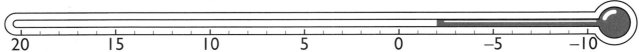

g If the thermometer drops by 15° what will the temperature be?

h If the thermometer rises by 18° what will the temperature be?

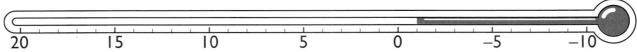

i If the thermometer drops by 12° what will the temperature be?

Refresher

1 Put each set of numbers in order from smallest to largest.

a 0, –6, 8, –2, –4, 3, 1, 7

b –1, –7, 2, –5, 7, 4, 0, –2

c –10, 5, 9, –2, 3, –8, 0, 1

d –3, –9, 0, 2, 6, 10, –5, –1

2 Look at each thermometer and answer the question.

a If the thermometer drops by 3° what will the temperature be?

b If the thermometer drops by 4° what will the temperature be?

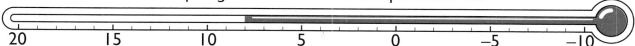

c If the thermometer rises by 7° what will the temperature be?

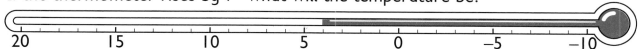

d If the thermometer rises by 11° what will the temperature be?

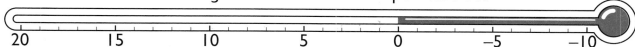

e If the thermometer drops by 8° what will the temperature be?

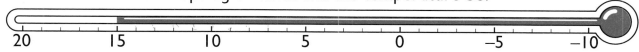

Challenge

1 Work out these calculations. Use the number line to help.

a 6 – 10

b 3 – 8

c 12 – 17

d 6 – 20

e 2 – 10

f 0 – 9

g 14 – 21

h 8 – 15

i 10 – 11

j 14 – 19

Multiplication and division facts

Practice

Knock any pins over and the numbers are multiplied together!

1 Write down the number on the blank pin.

a

36

Example
× 9 = 36

b

42

c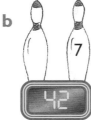

20

d

56

e

81

f

24

g

63

h

40

i

72

j

36

k

54

The scoreboards show your total score after each throw.

2 If you knock over two pins each time, write which pins could have been knocked over.

a 48   **b** 12   **c** 24   **d** 72   **e** 54

3 Knock over three pins each time.

a  100   **b** 8   **c** 30   **d**  42   **e**  120

Refresher

A multiplication square

1	2	3	4	5	6	7	8	9	10
11	12	13	14	15	16	17	18	19	20
21	22	23	24	25	26	27	28	29	30
31	32	33	34	35	36	37	38	39	40
41	42	43	44	45	46	47	48	49	50
51	52	53	54	55	56	57	58	59	60
61	62	63	64	65	66	67	68	69	70
71	72	73	74	75	76	77	78	79	80
81	82	83	84	85	86	87	88	89	90
91	92	93	94	95	96	97	98	99	100

You should know your times tables already, but you can check answers on a multiplication square.

1 Answer these using the multiplication square.

a 9×6 3×7 4×8 8×8

b 4×6 7×9 6×8 7×7

c 9×8 3×9 4×7 6×9

2 Find all of the multiplication facts that equal these numbers.

(32)   (81)   (24)   (40)   (54)

Challenge

Times it!

You need:
- $2 \times 1–12$ dice

- a pencil
- a scoresheet

A	B
500	500

Instructions

For 2 to 3 players

1 Draw up a score sheet with the players' names at the top. Give each player a starting number of 500.

2 Take turns to throw the two dice. Multiply the numbers together.

3 Subtract the answer from the start number to give a new total. Keep a running score.

4 The first person to reach 0 exactly is the winner.

Rounding remainders

Practice

Read each story. Write the division calculation and answer. If there is a remainder, think carefully whether you need to round your answer up or down.

a In one day 186 people went on the dodgem cars. Each dodgem car holds two people. How many times were the dodgem cars used?

b The rollercoaster seats four people per carriage. There are 298 people in the queue. How many carriages are required?

c Joshua has saved £58 to spend on rides. All rides cost £3. How many rides can he go on?

d The Fairy Floss stall made £125 in one day. Bags of Fairy Floss cost £2. How many bags were sold?

e Doughnuts are sold in packs of six. One batch of mixture makes 374 doughnuts. How many packs can be made up?

f The Youth Group has raised £467 for the day trip to the theme park. Entrance fees cost £9 per person. How many people can go?

g In one day 676 people went on the ghost train. Each carriage holds eight people. How many carriages were filled?

Refresher

Find the answers to these division problems. Be careful – some have remainders!

a $26 \div 4 =$

b $38 \div 5 =$

c $27 \div 3 =$

d $42 \div 5 =$

e $18 \div 2 =$

f $25 \div 3 =$

g $45 \div 6 =$

h $38 \div 7 =$

i $24 \div 6 =$

j $54 \div 6 =$

k $47 \div 7 =$

l $56 \div 7 =$

m $61 \div 9 =$

n $48 \div 8 =$

o $29 \div 9 =$

p $37 \div 9 =$

q $64 \div 8 =$

r $43 \div 8 =$

Challenge

Write your own word problems that involve rounding the answer up or down.

The arrow ↑ means to round the answer up.

The arrow ↓ means to round the answer down.

Choose five of the calculations below.

$327 \div 5$ ↑

$48 \div 9$ ↓

$124 \div 7$ ↑

$63 \div 10$ ↑

$264 \div 8$ ↓

$55 \div 6$ ↓

$74 \div 9$ ↑

$163 \div 7$ ↓

Fraction remainders

Practice

Read each problem.
Write a division calculation for each problem.
Record any remainders as a fraction.

a There are four children per group. Each group is given 13 chocolate cupcakes to share evenly between them. How many cakes do they get each?

b There are 74 chocolate biscuits to share between four groups. How many chocolate biscuits are there per group?

c There are 17 chocolate eclairs. Only five children like them. How many eclairs does each child receive?

d There are 25 packets of smarties to share equally between 10 children. How many packets does each child receive?

e The class teacher put aside 15 doughnuts to share with the staff for morning tea. There are 10 staff altogether. How many doughnuts per teacher?

f There are 47 smarties in each tube. Two children share each tube. How many smarties per child?

g There are 39 chocolate bars to share between four groups. How many chocolate bars per group?

h There are 5 children per group and 67 sweets per group. How many sweets are there per child?

Refresher

Copy and complete.

a   14 ÷ 3 = ⬚

b   32 ÷ 6 = ⬚

c   84 ÷ 9 = ⬚

d   61 ÷ 10 = ⬚

e   29 ÷ 4 = ⬚

f   43 ÷ 5 = ⬚

g   21 ÷ 7 = ⬚

h   19 ÷ 2 = ⬚

i   39 ÷ 6 = ⬚

j   37 ÷ 4 = ⬚

k   50 ÷ 8 = ⬚

l   32 ÷ 3 = ⬚

m   52 ÷ 6 = ⬚

n   72 ÷ 8 = ⬚

o   91 ÷ 9 = ⬚

p   54 ÷ 5 = ⬚

q   69 ÷ 6 = ⬚

r   32 ÷ 3 = ⬚

s   80 ÷ 8 = ⬚

t   66 ÷ 6 = ⬚

u   22 ÷ 4 = ⬚

Challenge

Hit the target

Use each set of cards shown. Make division calculations.
How close can you get to the target number?
Write your answers as a fraction.

Put a star beside the calculation that
gives the answer closest to the target.

Example

Target

6   7   9 → ◎ 10

$67 \div 9 = 7\frac{4}{9}$

$76 \div 9 = 8\frac{4}{9}$

*$69 \div 7 = 9\frac{6}{7}$

$79 \div 6 = 13\frac{1}{6}$

a   3   4   5   Target ◎ 7

b   6   7   8   Target ◎ 9

c   2   5   7   Target ◎ 3

d   7   9   8   Target ◎ 10

e   2   6   9   Target ◎ 3

f   3   6   8   Target ◎ 4

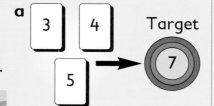

Money and decimals

Acorn School has 10 classes. They raised money to spend on books and games for each class.

Practice

Read each problem. Write a division calculation.
Give your answer.

a   Acorn School spent £474 on
dice and spinners for each class.
How much was spent per class?

b   The two Year 5 classes were given
£155 to spend on dictionaries.
How much is this per class?

c   The headteacher allocated £695 between
the 10 classes to be spent on games.
How much did each class receive?

d   The four infant classes spent £194 on
picture books for their reading corners.
How much was spent by each class?

e   A special discount applied if the school
purchased 10 hardback books. How much
was each book if the total cost was £81?

f   The school asked local businesses to donate money to the school.
Five businesses donated £236 between them. If each business
donated the same amount, how much did they each donate?

Refresher

Divide these amounts in pounds by the numbers given.
Give your answer in pence.

a   £1 ÷ 4 =

b   £1 ÷ 2 =

c   £1 ÷ 10 =

d   £1 ÷ 5 =

e   £2 ÷ 4 =

f   £3 ÷ 5 =

g   £2 ÷ 10 =

h   £4 ÷ 5 =

i   £3 ÷ 4 =

j   £5 ÷ 10 =

k   £3 ÷ 10 =

l   £2 ÷ 5 =

Challenge

Win or lose?

You need:
- money (notes and coins)
- blank die with the numbers 2, 2, 4, 4, 5, 10
- 10 cards with these amounts written twice: £1, £2, £3, £4, £5

Instructions

(For 2 to 4 players)
1 Shuffle the cards and place them face down in the centre of the table.
2 Take turns to select an amount card.
3 Take the required amount of money from the bank.
4 Roll the die. Divide your money by the number on the die using notes or coins from the bank.
5 Check with the other players to see if you are correct.

Multiplication and division lucky dip

Practice

Have a go at the Lucky Dip stall.

Choose the number of Lucky Dips as indicated.

a

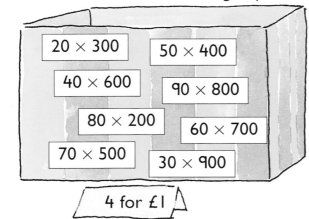

20 × 300	50 × 400
40 × 600	90 × 800
80 × 200	60 × 700
70 × 500	30 × 900

4 for £1

b

325 × 2	455 × 2
145 × 2	265 × 2
475 × 2	135 × 2
285 × 2	395 × 2

5 for £1

c

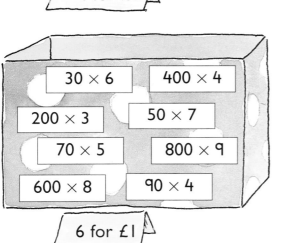

30 × 6	400 × 4
200 × 3	50 × 7
70 × 5	800 × 9
600 × 8	90 × 4

6 for £1

d

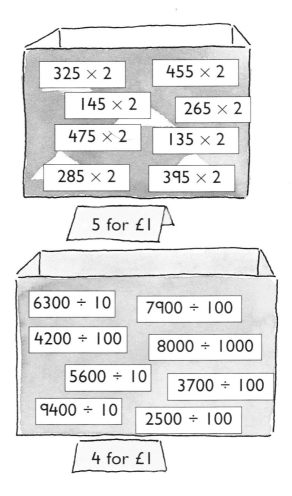

6300 ÷ 10	7900 ÷ 100
4200 ÷ 100	8000 ÷ 1000
5600 ÷ 10	3700 ÷ 100
9400 ÷ 10	2500 ÷ 100

4 for £1

e

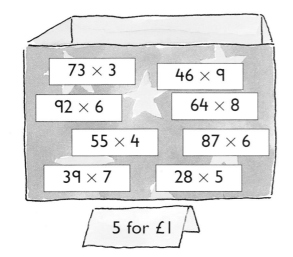

73 × 3	46 × 9
92 × 6	64 × 8
55 × 4	87 × 6
39 × 7	28 × 5

5 for £1

f

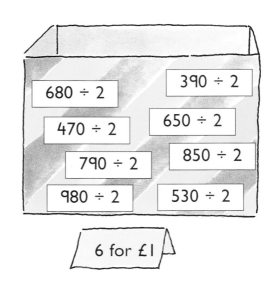

680 ÷ 2	390 ÷ 2
470 ÷ 2	650 ÷ 2
790 ÷ 2	850 ÷ 2
980 ÷ 2	530 ÷ 2

6 for £1

Refresher

The children bought tickets for the Lucky Dip stall.

The tickets show how many turns have been paid for and the price per turn.

The total cost on some tickets is incorrect. Find the incorrect tickets.

Write the calculation and the correct answer.

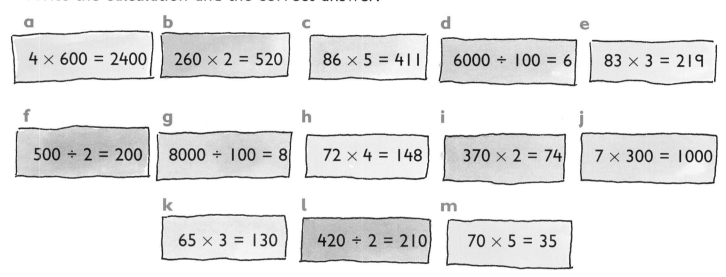

a $4 \times 600 = 2400$

b $260 \times 2 = 520$

c $86 \times 5 = 411$

d $6000 \div 100 = 6$

e $83 \times 3 = 219$

f $500 \div 2 = 200$

g $8000 \div 100 = 8$

h $72 \times 4 = 148$

i $370 \times 2 = 74$

j $7 \times 300 = 1000$

k $65 \times 3 = 130$

l $420 \div 2 = 210$

m $70 \times 5 = 35$

Challenge

Three children played a place value game.

They recorded their work on a place value chart.

They wrote their starter number in the correct position on the chart.

They turned over operation cards and recorded the answers until they reached their final score.

Find out who had the highest score.

Record your work on a place value chart.

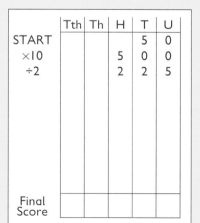

	Tth	Th	H	T	U
START				5	0
×10			5	0	0
÷2			2	2	5
Final Score					

Child 1 Start 50 ×10 → ÷2 → ÷2 → ×10 → ×2 → ÷100 → ×7 → ×2 → ×100

Child 2 26 ×6 → ×2 → ×10 → ÷2 → ÷2 → ÷2 → ÷10 → ×7 → ×100

Child 3 75 ×9 → ×2 → ×10 → ÷100 → ×2 → ×2 → ×100 → ÷10 → ×2

Doubling and halving

Practice

You know these doubling and halving strategies already.

To × 50
First
× 100
then halve

To × 16
First × 8
then double

To × 8
First × 4
then double

To × 5
First × 10
then halve

To × 20
First × 10
then double

It is easy to multiply by 12, 14 and 18 also.

Turn each number below into a number that is a known fact by halving.

When you get the answer, double it to get your final answer.

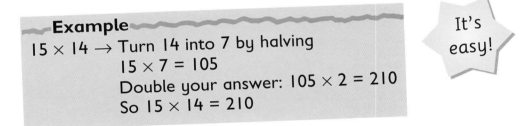

Example
$15 × 14 \rightarrow$ Turn 14 into 7 by halving
$15 × 7 = 105$
Double your answer: $105 × 2 = 210$
So $15 × 14 = 210$

It's easy!

Choose one number from each side. Multiply the two numbers together. Use a doubling or halving strategy from above to help you work out the answers.

Complete 20 calculations.

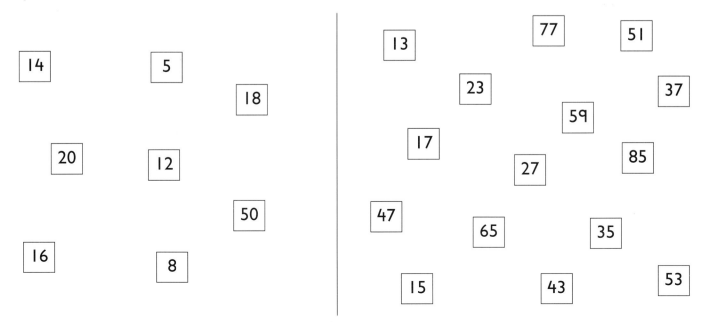

14   5
18
20   12
50
16   8

13   77   51
23   37
59
17   85
27
47   35
65
15   43   53

Refresher

Some numbers can be made easier to calculate with — by **doubling** or **halving**.
Find the numbers below that are easy to multiply by.
Write whether you would double or halve the number to help you
with a mental calculation.

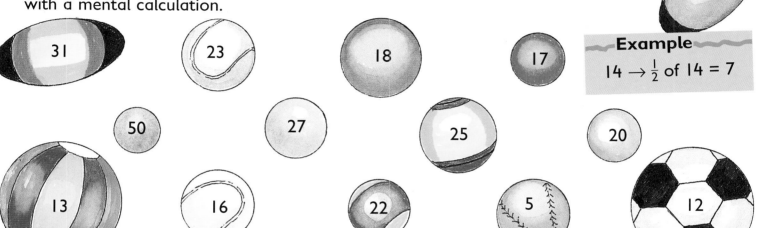

Example

$14 \rightarrow \frac{1}{2}$ of $14 = 7$

31   23   18   17   14

50   27   25   20

13   16   22   5   12

Challenge

'Easy multiplying' (It's like noughts and crosses)

You need:
● 6 counters each (one colour per person)

	Instructions

(For 2 players)
1 Choose two numbers from the labels on the left.
  Multiply them together using doubling or halving to help.
2 If your answer is on the grid, put a counter on that square.
3 The winner is the first person to get 3 in a row.

14   34   19

50   63   18

47   25   16

850	2350	288
1197	893	450
224	3150	476

21

Multiplication methods

Practice

1 Approximate the answer to each calculation.

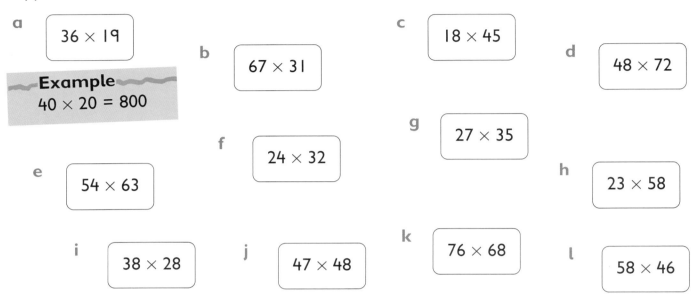

a 36×19

Example
$40 \times 20 = 800$

b 67×31

c 18×45

d 48×72

e 54×63

f 24×32

g 27×35

h 23×58

i 38×28

j 47×48

k 76×68

l 58×46

2 For each of the calculations above, use the grid method to work out the answer.
Match the answer to its calculation.

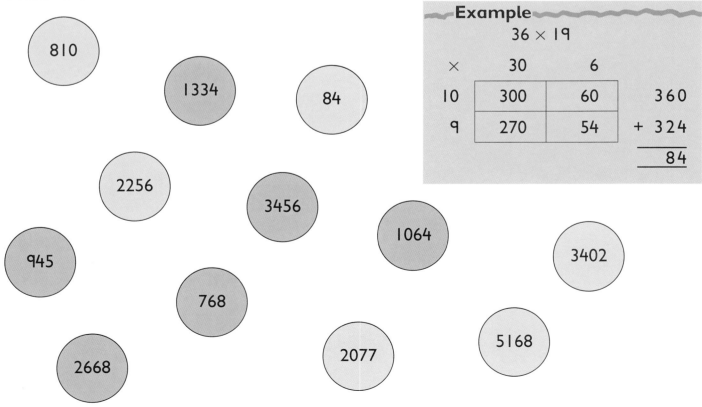

810

1334

84

2256

3456

1064

3402

945

768

5168

2077

2668

Example
36×19

×	30	6	
10	300	60	360
9	270	54	+ 324
			84

Refresher

Copy and complete.
Write the multiples of 10 each number is between.
Circle which multiple of 10 the number is closest to.

Example

70 ← 78 → (80)

a [ ] ← 46 → [ ]   f [ ] ← 54 → [ ]   k [ ] ← 57 → [ ]

b [ ] ← 93 → [ ]   g [ ] ← 61 → [ ]   l [ ] ← 78 → [ ]

c [ ] ← 39 → [ ]   h [ ] ← 17 → [ ]   m [ ] ← 64 → [ ]

d [ ] ← 25 → [ ]   i [ ] ← 33 → [ ]   n [ ] ← 96 → [ ]

e [ ] ← 82 → [ ]   j [ ] ← 85 → [ ]   o [ ] ← 73 → [ ]

Challenge

The multiplication game

You need:
- 12 counters each (one colour per person)
- a calculator (per person)

| 48 | 19 | 62 |

| 55 |

| 14 | 23 | 31 | 86 |

| Instructions |

(For 2 players)

1 Take turns to choose two factor cards above.
2 Multiply the two numbers together and choose an answer from the grid.
   Hint: Estimate the answer.
3 Check, using a calculator. If you are correct place a counter on the number.
4 Three in a row wins the game.

912	1705	1634
1265	2640	868
4730	322	1178
1104	5332	1922

More multiplication methods

Practice

1 Write multiplication facts for each box of numbers.

a
6   8
    7
  5
9   3

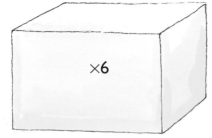

×6

b
  8   9
    3
  7
4   11

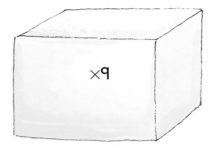

×9

c
  10   4
      6
  9
7
    8
  5

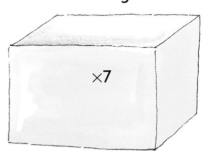

×7

2 Approximate your answer first.
Use the standard method of recording to work out the answer to each calculation.

Example

$72 \times 39 \rightarrow 70 \times 40 = 2800$

			7	2
		×	3	9
(72 × 30)	2	1	6	0
(72 × 9)		7	3	8
	2	8	9	8

a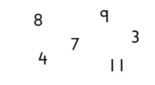
22 × 34

b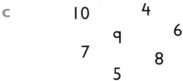
21 × 47

c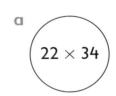
31 × 38

d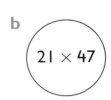
32 × 63

e
42 × 28

f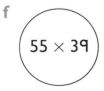
55 × 39

g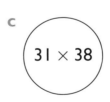
33 × 27

h
24 × 56

i
52 × 94

j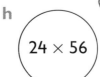
35 × 74

Remember
Keep the numbers in the correct columns!

24

Refresher

Choose five calculations. Approximate the answer first
then use the grid method to work out the answer.

 $20 \times 20 = 400$

a 16×27

b 33×22

Example

23×18

×	20	3
10	200	30
8	160	24

    230
+ 184
_____
    414

c 19×56

d 37×25

e 18×47

f 48×24

g 29×29

h 53×35

Challenge

1

| 2 | 4 | 5 | 6 |

Use each of these four digits once.
Arrange them to make a **product** as
close as possible to 1000.

☐ ☐ × ☐ ☐

or

☐ ☐ ☐ × ☐

2

| 3 | 5 | 7 | 9 |

Use each of these four digits once.
Arrange them to make a **product** as
close as possible to 5000.

☐ ☐ ☐ × ☐

or

☐ ☐ × ☐ ☐

Methods of calculating

Practice

1 Look at the calculations in the Refresher activity.
  Find the answers to the five easiest calculations.
  Work the answers out in your head.

2 For each of the calculations below work out the answer in two different ways.
  Show clearly the strategy you have used each time.

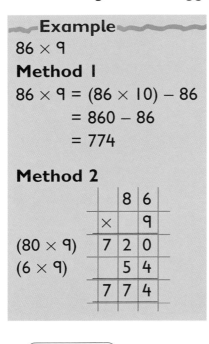

Example

86×9

Method 1

$86 \times 9 = (86 \times 10) - 86$
$\qquad\quad = 860 - 86$
$\qquad\quad = 774$

Method 2

		8	6
	×		9
(80 × 9)	7	2	0
(6 × 9)		5	4
	7	7	4

a 26×19 b $623 \div 7$ c 25×43

d $495 \div 9$ e 234×9 f 13×14

g 253×8 h 71×22 i 56×51

Refresher

1 Look carefully at the numbers in each calculation.
  For each pair of cards, decide which calculation is the easiest to work out.
  (Do not work out the answers.)

2 Explain your reasons.

a 26×19 | 26×91

b $357 \div 7$ | $456 \div 7$

c 231×9 | 319×2

d 66×39 | 96×63

e 8×51 | 8×43

f $356 \div 2$ | $356 \div 3$

g $480 \div 20$ | $263 \div 9$

h $809 \div 4$ | $609 \div 4$

i $845 \div 5$ | $752 \div 5$

j 49×30 | 63×30

Challenge

The **6** key on this calculator is missing.
To find out the answer to 36×23

I can do:

$$35 \times 23 = \quad 805$$
$$+ \ 1 \times 23 = \quad \underline{\ 23}$$
$$\underline{828}$$

Or I could do:

$$40 \times 23 = \quad 920$$
$$- \ 4 \times 23 = \quad \underline{\ 92}$$
$$\underline{828}$$

Use a calculator to find at least two ways of answering these:

a 76×52 **b** 116×33 **c** 264×20

d 68×39 **e** 66×23 **f** 39×666

g 1006×26 **h** 606×35 **i** 996×46

Solving word problems

Practice

Read the word problems. Choose an appropriate method of calculating your answer.
- Mental
- Mental with jottings
- Paper and pencil (standard method)

£2.50

£39

£28

£57

£23

a Mr Roberts buys five sets of golf clubs, one set for each of his children. The shop throws in one extra club per set. What is the value of the extra clubs?

b Jonathon buys a tennis racquet and a total of 12 tennis balls. What is the cost of his purchase?

c Netballs now cost half of their original price. How much money do you save by buying 16 balls in the sale?

d The golf club has three instructors. Each instructor has bookings for three-hour lessons and five $\frac{1}{2}$ hour lessons per day. Each instructor works seven days a week. How much money does the club take in golf lesson bookings in a week?

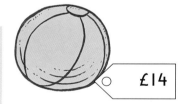

£14

e Mrs Jonson buys eight baseball bat sets for her class. How much change does she receive from £200?

£47

f The after-school club buys two of every item on sale, but not any golf lessons. How much do they spend?

Golf lessons
£13 per hour

Refresher

For each story decide which operation you will use to answer the question.
Work out the answer. Record the calculation.

a A set of three golf clubs costs £57 in the sale. How much does this work out per club?

b The golf instructor teaches 50 lessons a week. Each lesson costs £13. How much does he earn?

c The County Cricket Club buys 27 cricket balls for the season. Balls cost £14. How much does the club spend?

d The sports store has 100 tennis racquets on order. How much will they need to pay?

e Hockey sticks are sold by the manufacturer in boxes of 100. A box costs £3400. How much per stick?

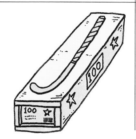

f Baseball gloves cost £25 each. The coach for the local club buys eight. How much does he spend?

Challenge

1 Use the prices of sports items on the opposite page to write your own word problems for these calculations.

2 Approximate the answer first (if necessary).

3 Calculate the answer using the most appropriate method. You may use a calculator.

a $(7 \times £2{\cdot}50) + (2 \times £39)$ b $(6 \times 56) + (12 \times 13)$ c $14 \times (\frac{1}{2} \times 13)$

d $(10 \times 47) - 47$ e $16 \times 23 + 47$ f $16 \times (23 + 47)$

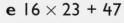
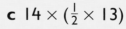
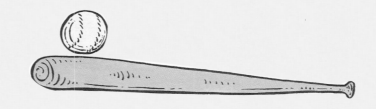

Decimals in order

Practice

1 Copy the number lines then put the decimals on them in the correct places.

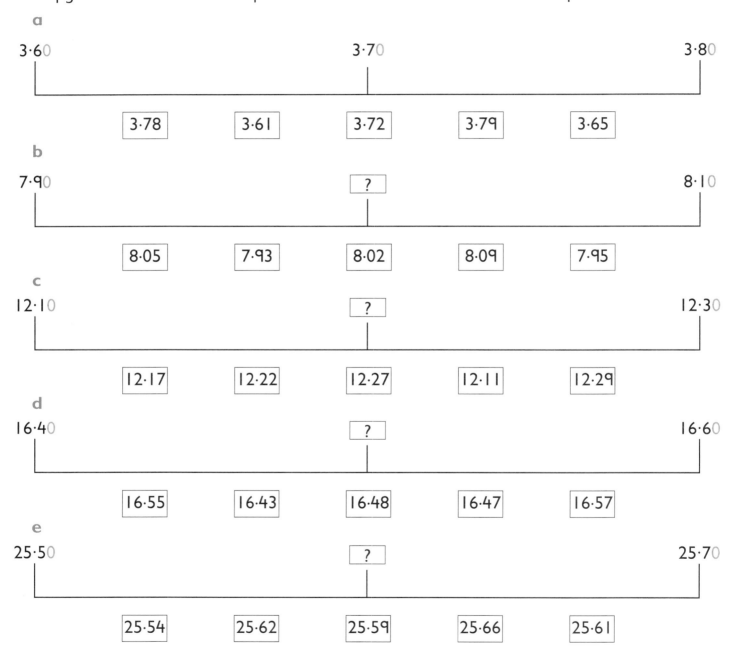

a

3·60   3·70   3·80

| 3·78 | 3·61 | 3·72 | 3·79 | 3·65 |

b

7·90   ?   8·10

| 8·05 | 7·93 | 8·02 | 8·09 | 7·95 |

c

12·10   ?   12·30

| 12·17 | 12·22 | 12·27 | 12·11 | 12·29 |

d

16·40   ?   16·60

| 16·55 | 16·43 | 16·48 | 16·47 | 16·57 |

e

25·50   ?   25·70

| 25·54 | 25·62 | 25·59 | 25·66 | 25·61 |

f Now add three more numbers onto each number line.

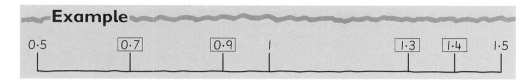

Refresher

Copy the number lines then put the decimals on them in the correct places.

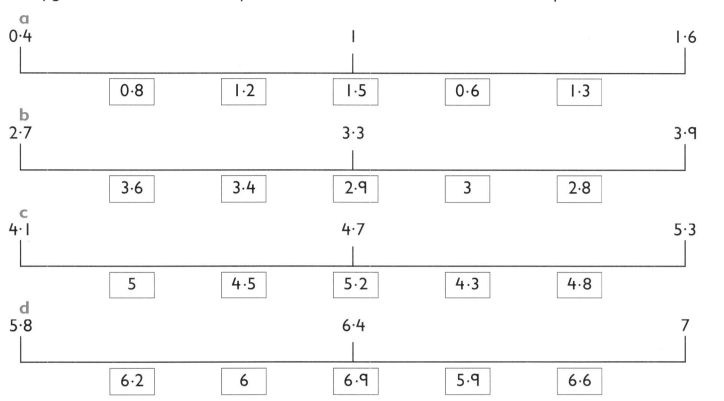

Challenge

1 Copy the number lines and then put the decimals on them in the correct places.

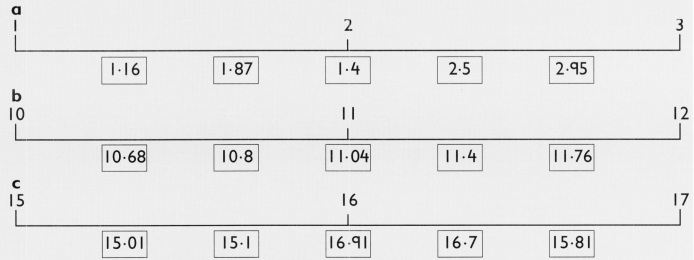

2 Now write a number **inbetween** the decimals on your number lines.

Change the decimal

Practice

1 Use the number lines to find the difference between the two decimals.
   Write your answer as a calculation.

a

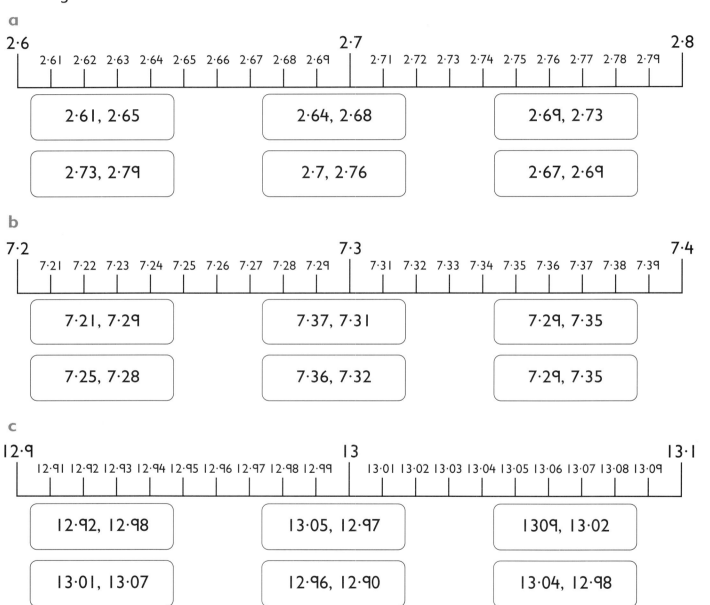

2·6 2·7 2·8

2·61 2·62 2·63 2·64 2·65 2·66 2·67 2·68 2·69 2·71 2·72 2·73 2·74 2·75 2·76 2·77 2·78 2·79

| 2·61, 2·65 | 2·64, 2·68 | 2·69, 2·73 |

| 2·73, 2·79 | 2·7, 2·76 | 2·67, 2·69 |

b

7·2 7·3 7·4

7·21 7·22 7·23 7·24 7·25 7·26 7·27 7·28 7·29 7·31 7·32 7·33 7·34 7·35 7·36 7·37 7·38 7·39

| 7·21, 7·29 | 7·37, 7·31 | 7·29, 7·35 |

| 7·25, 7·28 | 7·36, 7·32 | 7·29, 7·35 |

c

12·9 13 13·1

12·91 12·92 12·93 12·94 12·95 12·96 12·97 12·98 12·99 13·01 13·02 13·03 13·04 13·05 13·06 13·07 13·08 13·09

| 12·92, 12·98 | 13·05, 12·97 | 1309, 13·02 |

| 13·01, 13·07 | 12·96, 12·90 | 13·04, 12·98 |

2 Now change these decimals on the calculator. Record your operation.

   a Change 4·62 to 4·69.
   b Change 7·11 to 7·18.
   c Change 9·83 to 9·87.
   d Change 14·02 to 14·06.
   e Change 23·90 to 23·97.

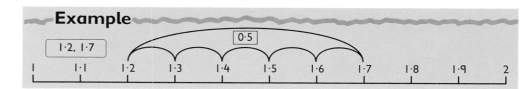

Example

1·2, 1·7

0·5

1   1·1   1·2   1·3   1·4   1·5   1·6   1·7   1·8   1·9   2

Refresher

Use the number lines to find the difference between the two decimals.
Write your answer as a calculation.

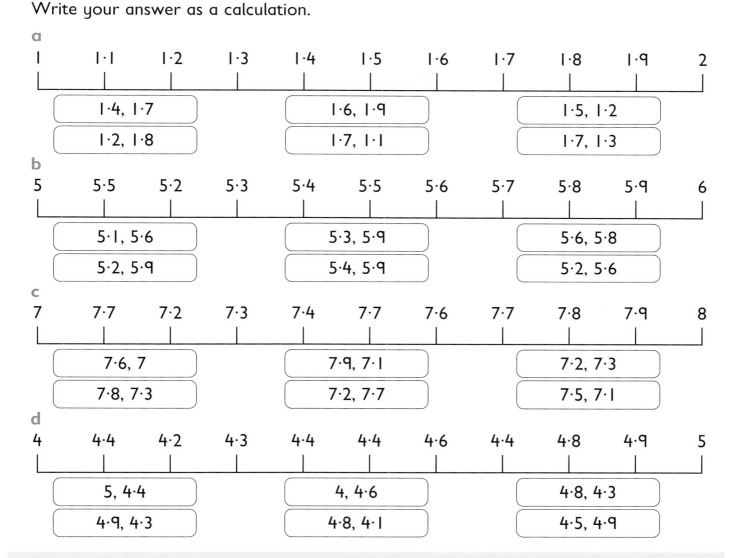

a

1   1·1   1·2   1·3   1·4   1·5   1·6   1·7   1·8   1·9   2

| 1·4, 1·7 | 1·6, 1·9 | 1·5, 1·2 |
| 1·2, 1·8 | 1·7, 1·1 | 1·7, 1·3 |

b

5   5·5   5·2   5·3   5·4   5·5   5·6   5·7   5·8   5·9   6

| 5·1, 5·6 | 5·3, 5·9 | 5·6, 5·8 |
| 5·2, 5·9 | 5·4, 5·9 | 5·2, 5·6 |

c

7   7·7   7·2   7·3   7·4   7·7   7·6   7·7   7·8   7·9   8

| 7·6, 7 | 7·9, 7·1 | 7·2, 7·3 |
| 7·8, 7·3 | 7·2, 7·7 | 7·5, 7·1 |

d

4   4·4   4·2   4·3   4·4   4·4   4·6   4·4   4·8   4·9   5

| 5, 4·4 | 4, 4·6 | 4·8, 4·3 |
| 4·9, 4·3 | 4·8, 4·1 | 4·5, 4·9 |

Challenge

Using a calculator change the first number to the second. Record your calculation.

a Change 8·6 to 86.   **b** Change 7·3 to 73.
c Change 61 to 6·1.   **d** Change 59 to 5·9.
e Change 1·3 to 13.   **f** Change 2·5 to 25.
g Change 36 to 3·6   **h** Change 99 to 9·9.
i Change 5·4 to 54.   **j** Change 0·6 to 6.

Up or down?

Practice

1 Using the digits on the cards, make up 10 numbers to one or two decimal places. Then round them to the **nearest** whole number.

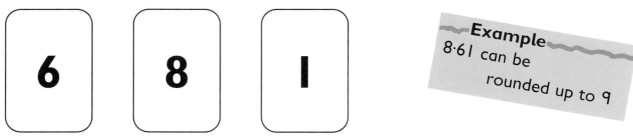

Example
8·61 can be rounded up to 9

2 Using the digits on the cards make up five numbers that can be rounded **down** to the nearest whole number.

3 Using the digits on the cards make up five numbers that can be rounded **up** to the nearest whole number.

Example

Is 6·81 nearer to 6 or 7?

6   6.5   6.81   7

4 Now make up 10 numbers for a friend to round up or down.

Refresher

Write down each decimal number.
Then write the two whole numbers that it comes between.
Circle the number that the decimal is closest to.

Example

6   6·8

a 6·8

b  5·1

c 2·7

d 8·3

e 4·9

f 5·4

g  18·5

h  12·7

i 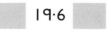 19·6

j  17·2

k  7·26

l 3·45

m  7·93

n  5·64

o 8·12

Challenge

Write down each decimal number. Then write the two whole numbers
that it comes between. Circle the number that the decimal is closest to.

a 4·268
b 6·782
c 1·586
d 9·106
e 2·688
f 0·999
g 3·783
h 7·226
i 5·314
j 2·891

Example
5·264
is between ⑤ and 6.

35

Find my partner

Practice

1 Match the decimals to their fraction partner.

$\frac{1}{4}$ 0·3

$\frac{3}{4}$ 0·74

$\frac{35}{100}$ 0·5

$\frac{21}{100}$ 0·75

$\frac{8}{10}$ 0·25

$\frac{1}{5}$ 0·35

$\frac{89}{100}$ 0·8

$\frac{1}{2}$ 0·89

$\frac{3}{10}$ 0·21

$\frac{74}{100}$ 0·2

2 Convert these fractions to their decimal equivalent.

a $4\frac{6}{10}$ b $8\frac{63}{100}$

c $24\frac{3}{4}$ d $45\frac{1}{2}$

e $34\frac{2}{100}$ f $18\frac{2}{5}$

g $28\frac{26}{100}$ h $20\frac{9}{10}$

i $33\frac{1}{4}$ j $41\frac{89}{100}$

3 Convert these decimals to their fraction equivalent.

a 5·64   b 3·78

c 9·4   d 24·5

e 11·06   f 26·75

g 14·2   h 20·42

i 3·09   j 26·7

Refresher

1 Match the decimals to their fraction partner.

0·5	$\frac{1}{10}$
0·1	$\frac{8}{10}$
0·8	$\frac{3}{10}$
0·2	$\frac{5}{10}$
0·6	$\frac{9}{10}$
0·9	$\frac{6}{10}$
0·4	$\frac{4}{10}$
0·7	$\frac{7}{10}$
0·3	$\frac{2}{10}$

2 Convert these decimals to their fraction equivalent.

4·5	6·7	8·1	5·3	4·7
12·8	14·6	9·2	15·4	17·9

Challenge

Find as many fractions as you can equivalent to these decimal fractions.

0·5   0·2   0·25   0·75

Fractions and decimals

Practice

1 Look at the number lines. What are the missing fractions and decimals?

a

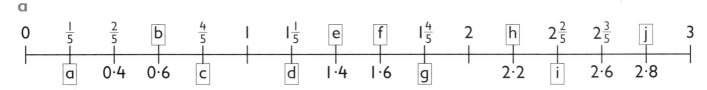

b

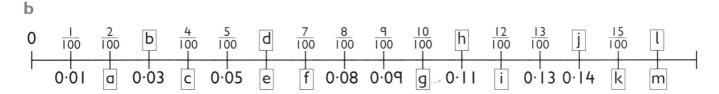

c

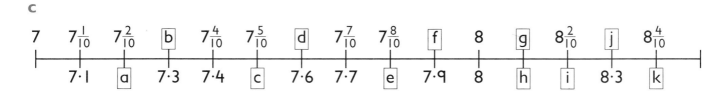

d

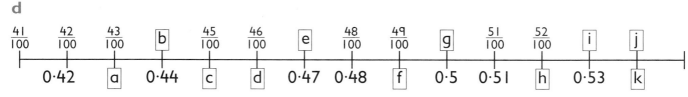

2 **Quick pointer**

Play with a friend.

Take it in turns to point to one of the fractions or decimals.

Your partner must point to the equivalent fraction or decimal.

You need:
● You need a sheet of A4 paper

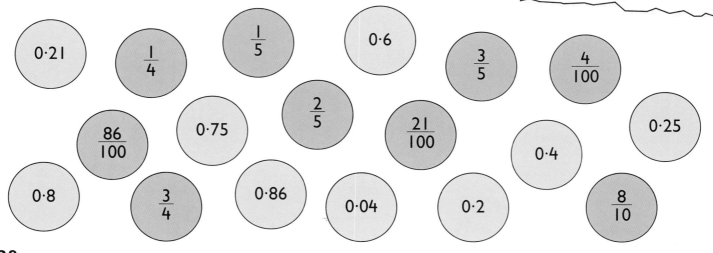

Refresher

1 Look at the number lines. What are the missing fractions and decimals?

a
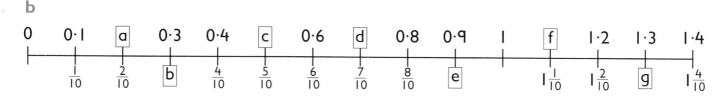

b
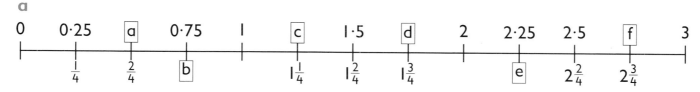

c
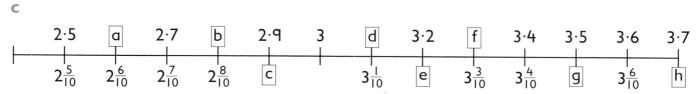

2 Quick pointer

Play with a friend.
Take it in turns to point to one of the fractions or decimals.
Your partner must point to the equivalent fraction or decimal.

You need:
● You need a sheet of A4 paper

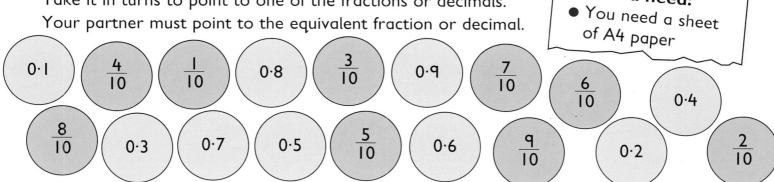

Challenge

What are the numbers?

    a I am thinking of a number: 0·2 of it is 12.
    b I am thinking of a number: $\frac{28}{100}$ of it is 14.
    c I am thinking of a number: 0·75 of it is 51.
    d I am thinking of a number: $\frac{6}{10}$ of it is 156.
    e I am thinking of a number: 0·25 of it is 34.

Fractions, decimals and percentages

Practice

Four in a row

You need:
- about 15 counters all the same colour
- two 1–6 dice

Instructions

(For 2 players)
1 Throw the dice and add up your score. Look at the grid and see which fraction or its equivalent that you can cover.
2 Choose a square to cover. The winner is the first person to get four counters in a row – horizontally, vertically or diagonally.

$\frac{3}{4}$	50%	$\frac{8}{10}$	60%	$\frac{3}{10}$
0·5	$\frac{1}{10}$	80%	0·2	10%
0·4	20%	0·1	$\frac{2}{10}$	0·25
$\frac{1}{4}$	0·7	$\frac{9}{10}$	0·6	$\frac{1}{2}$
0·8	40%	0·3	$\frac{6}{10}$	25%
0·75	$\frac{4}{10}$	75%	0·9	90%
$\frac{2}{10}$	70%	0·2	30%	$\frac{7}{10}$

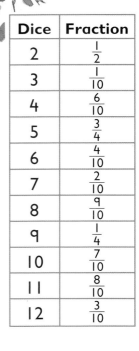

I've thrown 6 so I can cover $\frac{6}{10}$ or 40% or 0·4.

Dice	Fraction
2	$\frac{1}{2}$
3	$\frac{1}{10}$
4	$\frac{6}{10}$
5	$\frac{3}{4}$
6	$\frac{4}{10}$
7	$\frac{2}{10}$
8	$\frac{9}{10}$
9	$\frac{1}{4}$
10	$\frac{7}{10}$
11	$\frac{8}{10}$
12	$\frac{3}{10}$

40

Refresher

Look at each grid and write down what fraction and what percent is shaded.

I can see 80 squares are shaded so that is 80% or $\frac{1}{80}$.

Challenge

Work out the equivalent fractions and decimals for these percentages.

| 15% | 26% | 33% | 78% | 82% |
| 66% | 58% | 94% | 120% | 130% |

41

● Begin to understand percentage as the number of parts in every 100, and find simple
  percentages of small whole number quantities
● Express one half, one quarter, three quarters and tenths and hundredths as percentages

Fractions, decimals and percentages again

Practice

1 Copy and complete the table.

Fraction	Percentage	Decimal
	10%	
$\frac{75}{100}$		
		0·24
	80%	
		0·25
	20%	
		0·9
	40%	
		0·01
$\frac{53}{100}$		

2 Look at the percentages that are in **red**.
   They have another equivalent fraction. What is it?

Refresher

Choosing one sweet from each jar, match the equivalent fractions, decimals and percentages.

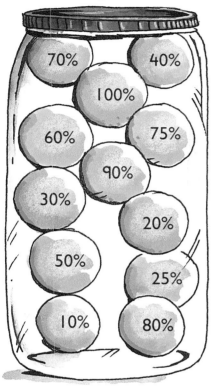
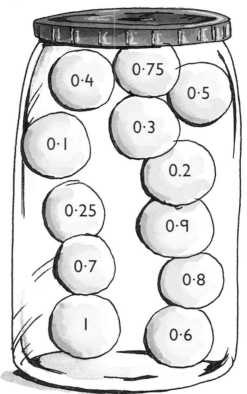
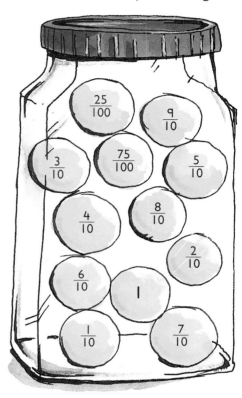

Challenge

Design a domino set where equivalent fractions and percentages are matched.
If you have time make the dominoes out of card and play the game.

Percentage problems

Practice

Work out the percentages. Show your working.

1 a 25% of £80

   b 25% of 44 m

   c 25% of £24

   d 25% of 60 kg

   e 25% of £10

2 a 50% of 26 cm

   b 50% of £48

   c 50% of 500 kg

   d 50% of £300

   e 50% of 150 m

3 a 10% of 40 m

   b 10% of £20

   c 10% of 200 cm

   d 10% of £150

   e 10% of £90

4 a 75% of £16

   b 75% of £40

   c 75% of 200 m

   d 75% of 80 kg

   e 75% of 60 minutes

5 Solve the percentage problems.

   a 70% of children at Woodlands School stay for lunch. What percentage do not stay?

   b 23% of children in Year 5 say maths is their favourite subject. How many do not like maths best?

   c A survey of favourite colours was done. 25% of people asked said red was their favourite colour and 14% said blue was their favourite. What percentage did not like red or blue best?

   d In a maths test I scored 40 marks out of 80 and my friend scored 45% of 80. Who did the best – me or my friend?

   e Richard and Sarah both have £30. Richard spends 20% of his money and Sarah spends £5. Who spent the most?

Refresher

1 Work out the percentages. Show your working.

   a 50% of 100 cm
   b 50% of £10
   c 50% of 100 kg
   d 50% of £1
   e 50% of 10 m

2 f 25% of £1
   g 25% of 100 m
   h 25% of £100
   i 25% of 100 kg
   j 25% of £10

3 k 10% of 100 m
   l 10% of £1
   m 10% of 100 cm
   n 10% of £100
   o 10% of £10

4 Solve the percentage problems.

   a 50% of the cake was eaten. What percentage was left?
   b 80% of the children in Year 5 walk to school. What per cent do not walk to school?
   c If I get 90% of questions right in a spelling test what per cent did I get wrong?
   d In a maths test I scored 60 out of 100. What per cent did I get?

Challenge

Make up five problems using these percentages for a friend to work out.

   a 25% of £148
   b 10% of 350
   c 60% of 30 km
   d 75% of 60 minutes
   e 40% of 120 g

Use the ratio

Practice

1 The sweets I buy always have two orange ones for every four red ones.
Copy and complete the table.

Orange	Red
2	4

a What is the ratio of orange sweets to red ones?

b How many red sweets would I have eaten if I had eaten 12 orange ones?

c How many orange sweets would I have if I had 32 red ones?

2 For every £2 pocket money I get my younger brother gets 50p.
Copy and complete the table showing our pocket money.

Me	My brother
£2	50p

a What is the ratio of my pocket money to my brother's?

b If my brother has £3 how much will I have?

c If we both save our money for eight weeks how much will we both have?

3 The recipe says that I need three eggs for every 10 cakes.
Copy and complete the table showing the ratio of eggs to cakes.

Eggs	Cakes
3	10

a What is the ratio of eggs to cakes?

b If I want to make 30 cakes how many eggs will I need?

c If I buy a dozen eggs how many cakes can I make?

Refresher

Fill in these tables.

a For every £1 Jack saves, his brother Joshua saves £3. Copy and complete the table showing their savings.

Jack	Joshua
£1	£3

b For every two boys in the class there are three girls. Copy and complete the table showing the boys and girls in the class.

Boys	Girls
2	3

c At home, for every two cakes that mum eats, dad eats four. Copy and complete the table showing how many cakes they eat.

Mum	Dad
2	4

Challenge

Answer these.

a I have bought 81 plants. Some are white and some pink. The ratio of pink to white plants is 2 to 7. How many of each colour plant do I have?

b I have 30 tomatoes so I can makes 6 litres of sauce. What is the ratio of tomatoes to sauce?

c I have two cats. One eats twice as much as the other. This week they have eaten 42 tins of food. How much did each cat eat?

In proportion

Practice

Work out the problems using the proportions given.
Draw a table to help you if you need to.

a Every box of biscuits has four chocolate biscuits for
   every five digestives. I buy a box of 36 biscuits. How
   many chocolate and how many digestives will I have?

b There are 63 children going on the school outing.
   every three boys going there are four girls. How
   many boys and how many girls are going?

c In every bag of apples you buy there are three re
   apples and five green. I buy four bags. How many
   and how many green apples will I have?

d In my savings box I have four 10 pences for every
   2 pences. Altogether I have 30 coins. How many 1
   pences and how many 2 pences do I have?

e On my necklace I have two round beads for every
   seven square beads. The necklace has 45 beads
   altogether. How many square and how many rou
   beads are there?

Refresher

Work out the problems. You may want to copy and complete the table to help you.

a The cat has three spoonfuls of food for every one the kitten has. I dished out 16 spoonfuls of food. How many does the cat have and how many does the kitten have?

Cat	Kitten	Total spoons
3	1	4

b Dad has made 25 cakes for him and me to eat. For each one he gives me, he has four. How many cakes do I get and how many does he get?

Me	Dad	Total cakes
1	4	5

c Every day I eat one apple for every two bananas. This week I have eaten 18 pieces of fruit. How many apples and how many bananas have I eaten?

Apples	Bananas	Total fruit
1	2	3

Challenge

I have counted all my T-shirts and altogether I have 50. For every two white T-shirts I have three grey ones.

a How many white T-shirts and how many grey T-shirts do I have?
b What fraction of my T-shirts are grey?
c What fraction of my T-shirts are white?
d What percentage of the T-shirts are grey?
e What percentage of the T-shirts are white?

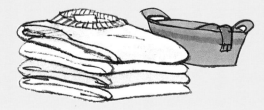

Dice bar line charts

Practice

1 Put your counter on the red dot. Roll your die to move the counter.

2 Record the numbers the counter touches in a table like the one below.

3 When you reach the blue dot, turn around and go back to the red dot.

4 Which number do you think you will land on most? Why?

5 Draw a bar line chart to show your results.

6	4	2	3	1	3	5	3	6	3
6	4	2	3	1	3	5	3	6	3
6	4	2	3	1	3	5	3	6	3
6	4	2	3	1	3	5	3	6	3
6	4	2	3	1	3	5	3	6	3
6	4	2	3	1	3	5	3	6	3

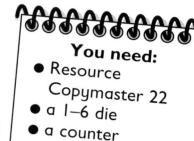

You need:
● Resource Copymaster 22
● a 1–6 die
● a counter

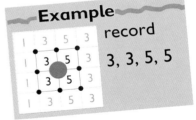

Example
record
3, 3, 5, 5

Number thrown	Tally	Total
1	2	3
2		
3		
4		
5		
6		

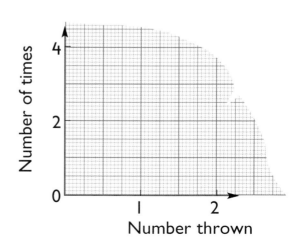

6 a Which number did you land on most?

b What is this number called?

c How many times did you land on a number above 3?

d Which number has the lowest frequency? How does your chart show this?

Refresher

1 Roll a die 40 times. Write down each number.

Die number	Number of rolls
1	
2	
3	
4	
5	
6	

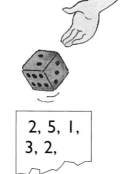

2, 5, 1, 3, 2,

2 Count how many times you rolled each number.
   Copy and complete the table.

3 Copy and complete the bar line chart using
   Resource Sheet 22.

4 a How many times did you roll a 3?
   b Which number did you roll the most?
   c What is this number called?
   d How many times did you roll a 1 or 6?

You need:
● Resource Copymaster 22
● a die

(Graph: Number of rolls (vertical axis, 0–10) vs Die number (horizontal axis, 1–6))

Challenge

Work in a group.

1 Take turns to empty the box of dice.
   Record the results in a tally chart.

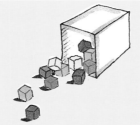

2 Each person draws a bar line chart using Resource Sheet 22.
3 a What is the mode?
   b What is the frequency of the mode?
   c How many numbers greater than the mode
      were rolled?
   d How many numbers less than the mode were rolled?
4 If you emptied the box of dice again, which number
   do you think would come up most?
   Try it and see.

You need:
● Resource Copymaster 22
● a box of 1–6 dice

Die number	Tally	Total
1	//	
2	//// /	
3	///	
4	///	
5	////	
6	//	

Travel line graphs

Practice

The diagram shows a school trip.

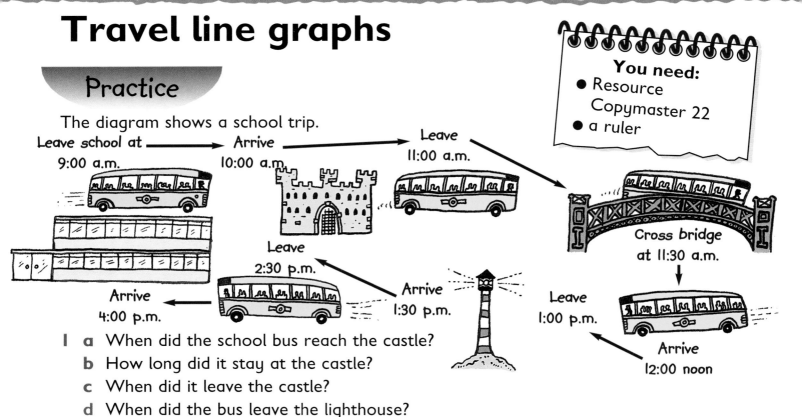

You need:
● Resource Copymaster 22
● a ruler

1 a When did the school bus reach the castle?
  b How long did it stay at the castle?
  c When did it leave the castle?
  d When did the bus leave the lighthouse?
  e Where was the bus at 2:30 p.m.?

2 Copy and complete this line graph. Use Resource Copymaster 22.

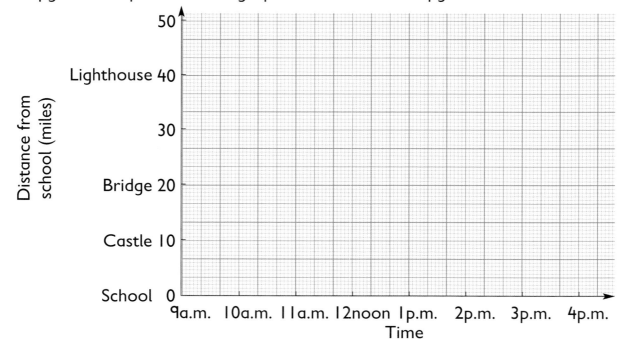

3 a How far is the bridge from the school?
  b How far did the bus travel altogether?
  c How long did the school trip last?
  d How far from school was the bus at 9:30 a.m.?

52

Refresher

Nazir delivers pizzas on his motorbike. The line graph shows his journey.

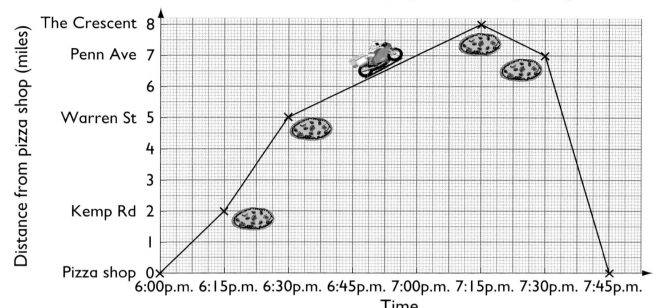

a Where did Nazir deliver his first pizza? At what time was this?
b Where did he deliver his next pizza? When was this?
c When did he deliver a pizza at Penn Avenue?
d Did he deliver a pizza at 7:15 p.m.?
e When did he start back to the pizza shop?
f How far is The Crescent from the pizza shop?

Challenge

The line graph shows the journey an aeroplane made one day.

Describe the journey. Begin like this: 'Took off from London at 8:00 a.m.'

53

Ranges of clothes sizes

Practice

1 Calculate the range of shoe sizes for each colour.

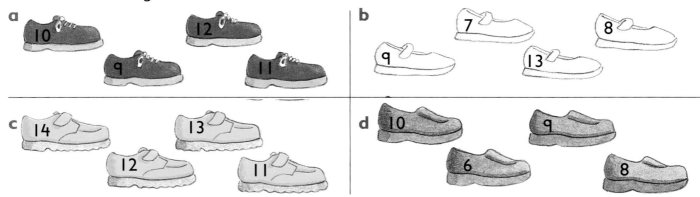

a 10 12 9 11

b 7 8 9 13

c 14 13 12 11

d 10 9 6 8

2 Which colour has the widest range of sizes?

3 Calculate the range of sizes for each brand.

a 34 28 RANCHO 27 36

b 34 32 Bells 41 37 36

c 29 32 Devi 27 42

d 35 30 36 Spiros 40 31

4 Which brand has the narrowest range of sizes?

5 Calculate the range of sizes each shop has for sale.

a $12\frac{1}{2}$ $15\frac{1}{2}$ 16 13 THE HUT

b 18 15 $16\frac{1}{2}$ $14\frac{1}{2}$ POOLS

c 16 $17\frac{1}{2}$ 15 $13\frac{1}{2}$ TOP GEAR

d $12\frac{1}{2}$ $13\frac{1}{2}$ $14\frac{1}{2}$ $16\frac{1}{2}$ FLAIR

6 Which shop sells the widest range of sizes?

54

Refresher

1 Calculate the range of sizes.

a

 2
 2
 3
 4
 4
 5

b

 28
 28
 30
 34
37
39

2 a What is the smallest dress size?
 b What is the largest dress size?
 c Calculate the range.

 18
 17
 13
 9
 15
 21
 15
16

Challenge

Fill in the missing size. The range is given for each set.

a Range = 4  1   2

b Range = 5  38   40

c Range = 3 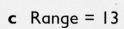 $15\frac{1}{2}$ $16\frac{1}{2}$

d Range = 10 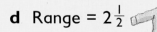 19   11

e Range = 3  11   9

f Range = 9  35   31

2 Make up your own sizes that have the given range.

a Range = 7

b Range = 3

c Range = 13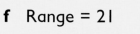

d Range = $2\frac{1}{2}$

e Range = 1

f Range = 21

55

Ticket inspection

Practice

1 Find the mode for each set of ticket prices.

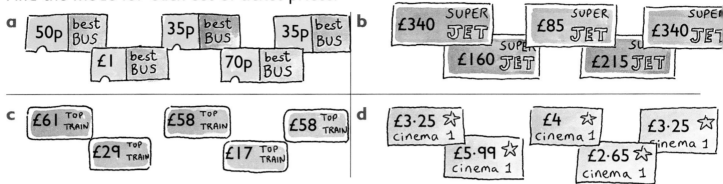

a
50p best BUS   35p best BUS   35p best BUS
£1 best BUS   70p best BUS

b
£340 SUPER JET   £85 SUPER JET   £340 SUPER JET
£160 SUPER JET   £215 JET

c
£61 TOP TRAIN   £58 TOP TRAIN   £58 TOP TRAIN
£29 TOP TRAIN   £17 TOP TRAIN

d
£3·25 ☆ cinema 1   £4 ☆ cinema 1   £3·25 ☆ cinema 1
£5·99 ☆ cinema 1   £2·65 ☆ cinema 1

2 Calculate the range for the ticket prices in question 1.

3 Find the mode for each set of ticket prices.

a

Cinema ticket	Number of tickets
£5	3
£6	9
£7	24
£8	30
£9	15
£10	7

b

Taxi fare	Number of tickets
£1·50	0
£2·00	6
£2·50	11
£3·00	9
£3·50	11
£4·00	16

c

Aeroplane ticket	Number of tickets
£90	34
£130	42
£200	16
£240	5
£275	3
£340	0

4 Calculate the range for the above ticket prices.

5 Which coach company has the biggest mode of prices?

  a Express Coaches

  b Lux Tours

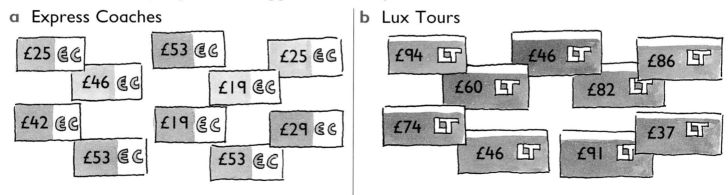

a Express Coaches
£25 EC   £53 EC   £25 EC
£46 EC   £19 EC
£42 EC   £19 EC   £29 EC
£53 EC   £53 EC

b Lux Tours
£94 LT   £46 LT   £86 LT
£60 LT   £82 LT
£74 LT   £37 LT
£46 LT   £91 LT

6 Which coach company has the biggest range of prices?

Refresher

1 Find the mode for each set of ticket prices.

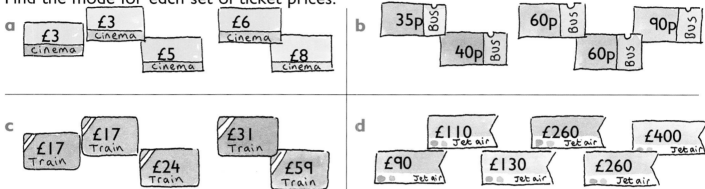

a
£3 Cinema
£3 Cinema
£5 Cinema
£6 Cinema
£8 Cinema

b
35p Bus
40p Bus
60p Bus
60p Bus
90p Bus

c
£17 Train
£17 Train
£24 Train
£31 Train
£59 Train

d
£110 Jet air
£90 Jet air
£260 Jet air
£130 Jet air
£400 Jet air
£260 Jet air

2 Calculate the range for each set of prices.

Challenge

Work in pairs. You will need a 0–9 die.

1 Each person rolls the die 10 times.
  Multiply the numbers by 10 to get bus fares.

Example
$4 \times 10 = 40p$ bus fare

2 Calculate the mode and range for your own set of fares.

3 Compare your sets of fares.

4 Do it again. This time, roll the die twice to get two-digit prices.
  Calculate the range. Compare your sets of fares.

The bus fare is 63p.

5 Do it again. This time, roll the die three times to get £ and p prices.
  Calculate the range. Compare your sets of fares.

The bus fare is £2·94.

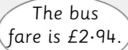

Collecting for school computers

Practice

You need:
● Resource Copymaster 22
● a ruler

These children collected money each month for school computers.

Marcus			Jane			Pritam	
Nov.	£14		Nov.	£20		Oct.	£10
Dec.	£26		Dec.	£35		Nov.	£15
Jan.	£8		Jan.	£10		Dec.	£10
Feb.	£40		Mar.	£20		Feb.	£15
Mar.	£14		Apr.	£20		Mar.	£10
			May	£5		Apr.	£5

1 For each person, find the mode of the amounts collected.
   Which person has the greatest mode?

2 For each person, find the range. Which person has the greatest range?

3 Find the amount collected each month by the children.
   Copy and complete the table.

Month	Amount collected £
Oct.	
Nov.	
Dec.	
Jan.	

4 Copy and complete the line chart. Use Resource Copymaster 22.

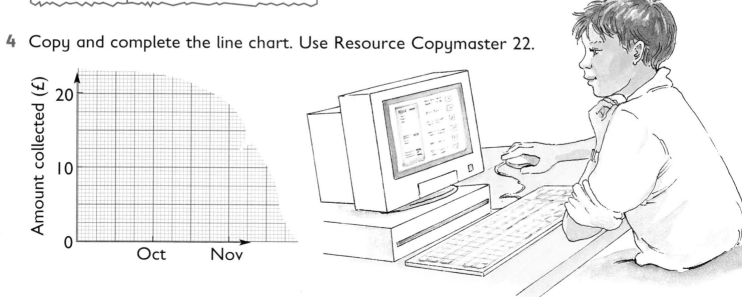

Refresher

1 The line graph shows the money collected for school computers each month.

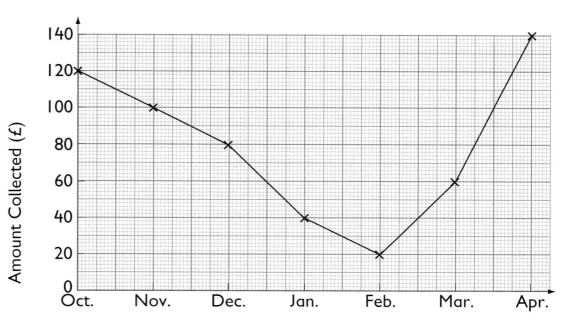

a How much was collected in March?

b When was £40 collected?

c When did the money collected stop falling?

d In which months was more than £50 collected?

2 Copy and complete the table.

Month	Amount collected £
Oct.	
Nov.	
Dec.	

Challenge

You will need Resource Copymaster 00.

These amounts of money were given by parents for school computers.

Sept. £1 £2 £2·50	**Jan.** 50p £2 £2·50 £3
Oct. 50p £2·50 £2·50 £3	**Feb.** £1 £1 £1·50 £2·50 £3
Nov. £1·50 £1·50 £2·50	**Mar.** 50p £1·50 £2·50 £3
Dec. 50p 50p £1 £1	**Apr.** £2 £2·50 £3

a Find the mode and range.

b Draw a line graph to show the money collected each month.

c Draw a bar line chart to show the amounts given.

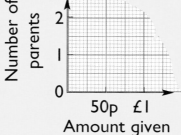

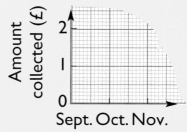

59

Calculating costs

Practice

£6·48   £4·25   £8·52   96p

1 Use your calculator to find the total cost. Write down your working.

   a A calculator and two filofaxes

   b Three computer mice and a stapler

   c Two filofaxes and two computer mice

   d Five staplers and 4 calculators

   e Two computer mice, two filofaxes and two calculators

   f Five of each item

2 Now work out these.

   a How much more is a mouse than a filofax?

   b How much more are three filofaxes than a mouse?

   c How much more is a calculator than a stapler?

   d How much more are seven staplers than a filofax?

3 Calculate the cost in two different ways.

 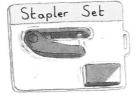 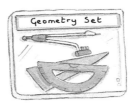

pen £1·34   stapler £2·28   compasses £1·97
pencil 90p   staples 75p   protractor 75p

   a Four geometry sets

   b Two pen and pencil sets

   c Three stapler packs

   d Four geometry sets and a stapler pack

   e Five pen and pencil sets and two stapler packs

Example

Find the cost of two geometry sets

Two compasses cost

    $2 \times £1·97 =$ £3·94

Two protractors cost

    $2 \times 75p =$ £1·50

Total cost   £5·44

Compasses and protractor cost

    £1·97 + 75p = £2·72

2 geometry sets cost

    $2 \times £2·72 =$ £5·44

Refresher

 £65    £27    £58    £327

1 Use your calculator to find the total cost. Write down your working.

 a Two mobile phones and a printer
 b Three telephones and a computer
 c Four printers, a computer and telephone
 d Two mobile phones and three printers

2 Use your calculator to find the total cost in £ and p. Write down your working.

27p   48p   92p   83p

 a Four pencils and an eraser
 b A sharpener and three rulers
 c Two erasers and two pencils
 d Five sharpeners and two rulers

Challenge

1

 £29    £44    £53   £19

Try both methods to find the cost of these items. When does the quick method work?

 a Three satchels and a suitcase
 b A handbag and three briefcases
 c A briefcase and two suitcases
 d Five suitcases and a satchel

2 Write down a rule for when the quick method works.

Example
Find the cost of four handbags and a suitcase.
Usual method
Four handbags cost
$4 \times £19 =$ £76
A suitcase costs   £53
Total cost =   £129

Quick method
Four handbags and
a suitcase cost:
$4 \times £19 + £53$

[4] [×] [1] [9] [+] [5] [3] [=]   129.

Total cost = £129

61

Calculator error

Practice

1 Work out each calculation using your calculator.
   Write the answer on your calculator display.
   Write the exact answer.

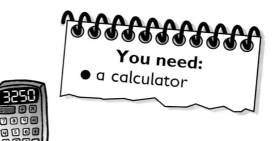

You need:
● a calculator

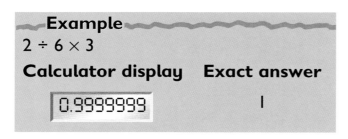

Example
2 ÷ 6 × 3

Calculator display	Exact answer
0.9999999	1

a 4 ÷ 3 × 3   b 2 ÷ 3 × 12   c 8 ÷ 12 × 3

d 25 ÷ 15 × 3   e 7 ÷ 6 × 18   f 32 ÷ 48 × 6

g 250 ÷ 90 × 9   h 11 ÷ 12 × 36   i 10 ÷ 30 × 15

j 64 ÷ 48 × 6   k 17 ÷ 9 × 72   l 500 ÷ 300 × 150

m 1000 ÷ 90 × 900   n 2 ÷ 600 × 1800

2 Work out the first part of each calculation using your calculator.
   Find the missing number that gives the answer. Choose from:
   3   6   9   12   15   24   30

a 4 ÷ 3 × = 12   b 8 ÷ 12 × = 2   c 5 ÷ 6 × = 10

d 2 ÷ 3 × = 20   e 10 ÷ 3 × = 40   f 8 ÷ 6 × = 32

g 40 ÷ 72 × = 5   h 7 ÷ 3 × = 35   i 200 ÷ 24 × = 100

3 Make up your own calculation.
   Write any number in the box.
   Work out the exact answer.

a ÷ 3 × 15   b ÷ 6 × 60   c ÷ 3 × 9

d ÷ 9 × 36   e ÷ 60 × 120   f ÷ 45 × 900

Refresher

1 These calculators have made a rounding error.
Write down the correct answer.

a `2.9999998` b `0.9999999` c `21.999999`

d `10.999998` e `9.9999999` f `50.999999`

g `46.999999` h `29.999999` i `99.999999`

2 Calculate the answer. Round it to the nearest whole number.

a 8×1.999999 b 7×9.9999999

c 25×0.9999999 d 11×10.9999999

e 2×19.999999 f 9×99.999999

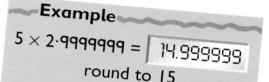

Example

$5 \times 2.9999999 =$ `14.999999`

round to 15

Example

Wendy buys nine pieces.

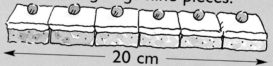

20 cm

Length of one piece = $20 \div 6$
Length of nine pieces = $20 \div 6 \times 9$
$29.99999 = 30$ cm

Challenge

You will need a calculator.

A baker cuts her cakes into equal pieces.
Find the total length of the pieces bought.
Write down your calculation.

a Barry buys 15 pieces.

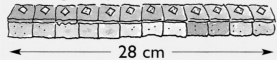

26 cm

b Prakesh buys nine pieces.

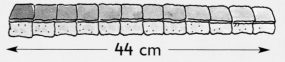

32 cm

c Karen buys 18 pieces.

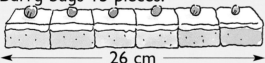

40 cm

d Hans buys 36 pieces.

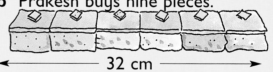

25 cm

e Mel buys 18 pieces.

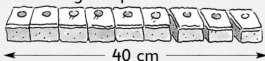

28 cm

f Jo buys 21 pieces.

44 cm

Checking calculations

Practice

1 Work out each calculation using your calculator.

   a 59×11 b $607 - 395$ c 21×38

   d $489 \div 992$ e $288 \div 9$ f 22×71

   g $608 \div 19$ h $1207 - 592$ i $1805 \div 95$

2 Check your answers to question 1.
   Work out a rough calculation.
   Show your working.

> **Example**
> Calculator: $31 \times 19 = 589$
> Rough calculation: $30 \times 20 = 600$
> The two answers are close, so the
> calculator answer is probably correct.

3 Work out each calculation using your calculator.

   a $258 + 673$ b 93×48 c $2007 \div 9$

   d $972 - 359$ e $1944 \div 54$ f 112×17

   g $5329 - 1842$ h 88×88 i $9000 - 4621$

4 Check your answers to question 3.
   Work backwards. Show your working.

> **Example**
> Calculator $1368 \div 57 = 24$
> Work backwards $24 \times 57 = 1368$
> The answer is correct.

5 Use your calculator to answer these questions.
   Check each answer using the most efficient method.

   a How long are 23 skipping
      ropes joined together?

      1·83 m

   b How much more expensive
      is the blue bicycle?

      £60·21   £38·77

   c How much drink does each person get?

 Jungle
   juice
   4320 ml

   d How far is Thurso from Exeter?

      371 miles   352 miles

      ●————————————●————————————●
      Thurso   Carlisle   Exeter

   e The cost of 11 cakes is £16·28.
      How much does one cake cost?

   f There are 250 envelopes in a box.
      How many in 17 boxes?

Refresher

1 Round these numbers to the nearest 10.

   a 87   b 23   c 11   d 18   e 72

2 Round these numbers to the nearest 100.

   a 203   b 396   c 187   d 509   e 93

3 Round these numbers to the nearest 1000.

   a 1992   b 3020   c 2106   d 4851   e 962

4 Work out each calculation using your calculator.
   Repeat the calculation to check your answer.

   a 27×16 b $450 - 279$ c $586 \div 8$

   d $821 + 598$ e 69×11 f $3306 \div 58$

Challenge

1 Work out each calculation using your calculator.

   a $19 \times 9 - 61$ b $493 + 712 - 385$

   c $936 \div 18 + 108$ d $21 \times 31 - 405$

   e $2142 + 6060 - 3951$ f $29 \times 39 \times 9$

   g $3504 \div 48 - 29$ h $103 \times 62 + 986$

2 Check your answers to question 1.
   Work out a rough calculation.

3 Use your calculator to answer these questions.
   Check each answer using the best way.

   a Calculate the total cost.

      £8125   £6999   £9852

   b Calculate the cost of nine shampoos
      and a sponge.

      £1·82   £3·10

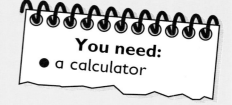

You need:
● a calculator

Example
Calculator $38 \times 96 - 982 = 2666$
Rough calculation $40 \times 100 - 1000$
                $= 4000 - 1000 = 3000$
Fairly close, so calculator answer is
probably correct.

Reflective symmetry

Practice

1 **a** Cut out the remaining four regular polygons on Resource Copymaster 00.

   b By folding only, find and draw the axes of symmetry in each polygon.

   c Copy and complete the table.

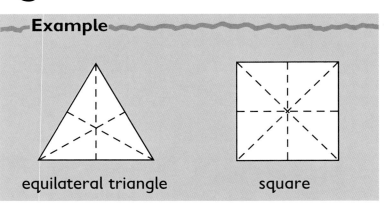

Example

equilateral triangle   square

Regular polygon	Number of		
	equal sides	equal angles	axes of symmetry
Equilateral triangle	3	3	3
Square			
Pentagon			
Hexagon			
Heptagon			
Octagon			

2 Use your findings in the table to work out these.

Regular polygon	Number of		
	equal sides	equal angles	axes of symmetry
9-sided			
10-sided			
11-sided			
12-sided			

3 Copy and complete this general statement:

The number of lines of symmetry in a regular polygon is equal to ...

Refresher

Draw each irregular quadrilateral on squared paper and cut out the shape.

Test each shape for symmetry by using a mirror and by folding.

Draw the lines of symmetry with a ruler.

Paste the shapes into your exercise book.

Example

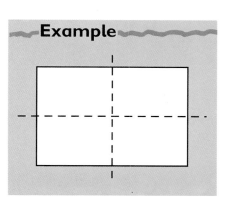

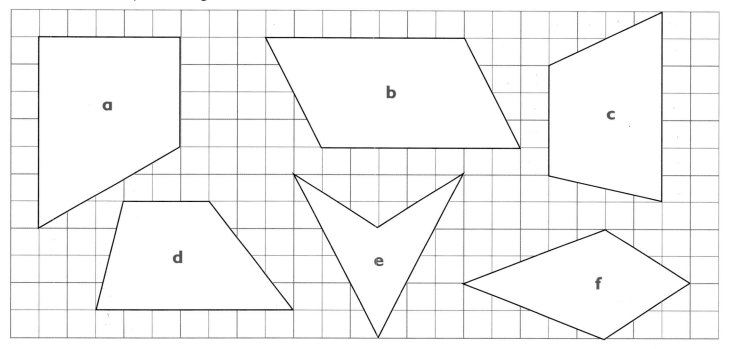

Challenge

If you add different regular polygons together to make a pattern, will you change the number of axes of symmetry of the regular polygon at its centre? Investigate.

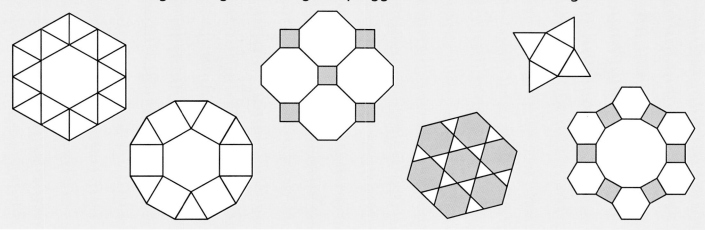

67

Symmetrical patterns

Practice

1 Copy each grid on to squared paper.
Draw the two lines of symmetry with dotted lines.
Mark the position of each peg as shown.
Reflect each peg, in turn, into the other
three sectors and complete your pattern.

Example

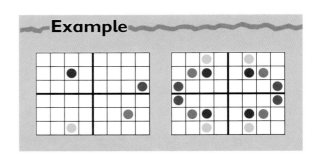

Hint: Choose a different colour
for each peg.

a
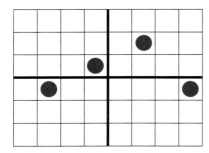

b
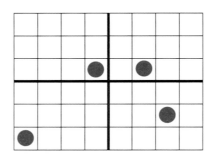

c
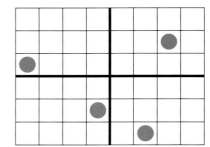

d
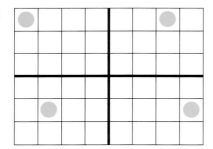

e
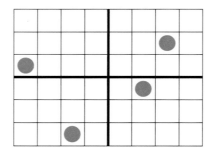

f
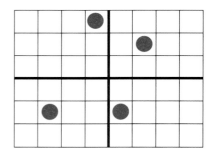

2 Copy and complete these patterns made by squares and triangles.

a
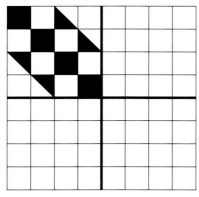

b
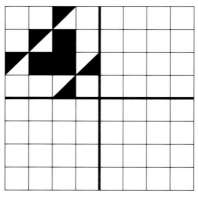

Refresher

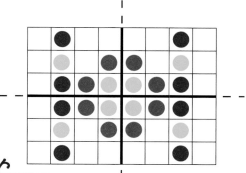

1 Check that this pattern has two lines of symmetry.
   Place your mirror on the dotted lines.

2 Copy each grid on to squared paper.
   Draw the two lines of symmetry with dotted lines.
   Use four colours.
   Reflect and complete each pattern.

Remember

Check with
a mirror.

a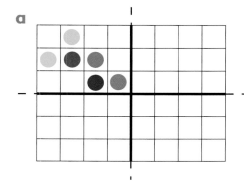

b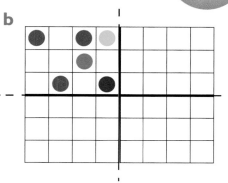

c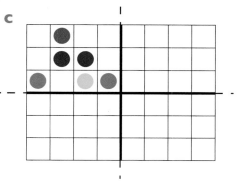

Challenge

Choose a grid paper and four colours.
Make a pattern with two axes of symmetry.

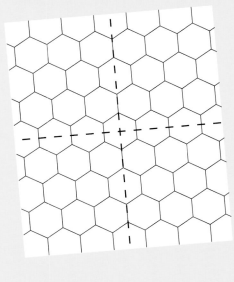

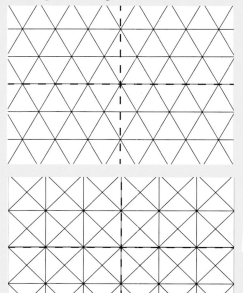

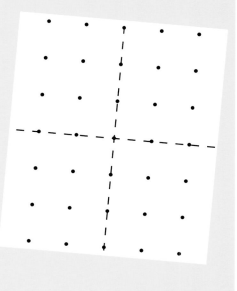

Reflecting 2D shapes

Practice

Copy each shape and dotted mirror line on to squared paper.
Using the mirror line, find and draw the reflected shape.

Example

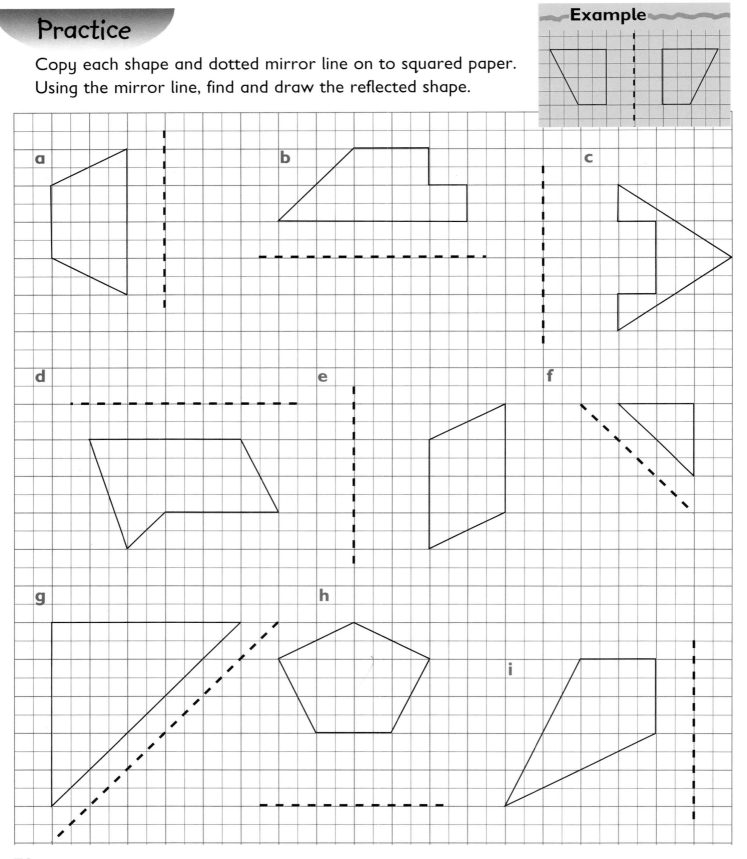

Refresher

For each word decide whether the reflections are true or false.
Use your mirror to check.

a

b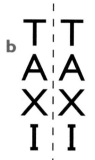

c HANNAH|HANNAH

d BETH|HT38

e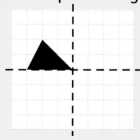

f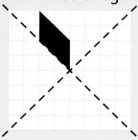

g

Challenge

Copy each shape on to squared paper.
Complete the pattern by reflecting the shape in both axes of symmetry.

a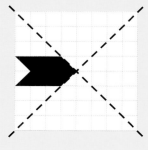

b

c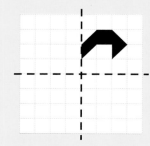

d

71

Making an Islamic pattern

Practice

1 On dot paper, outline a 6 × 6 square.

2 Copy steps 1, 2 and 3 on to your square.
Draw all your lines lightly in pencil.
Some will be rubbed out later.

3 Look at step 3 and find the lines which were used to make these four patterns.

4 a Copy one of the patterns on to your square.

   b Using a symmetrical plan, colour your pattern.

   c Now design your own Islamic pattern.

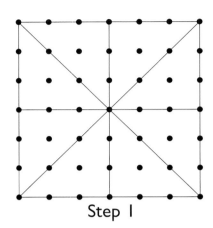

Step 1

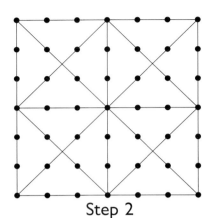

Step 2

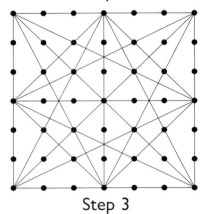

Step 3

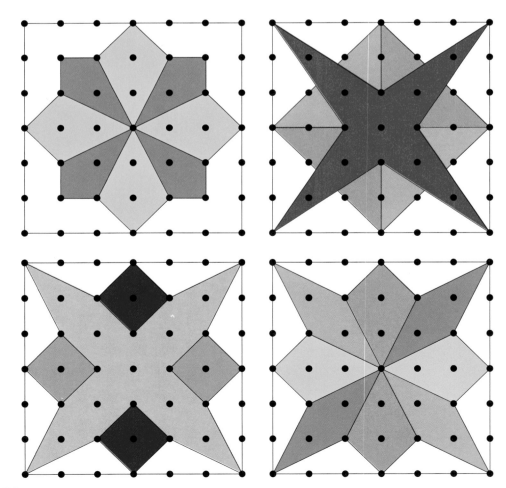

Refresher

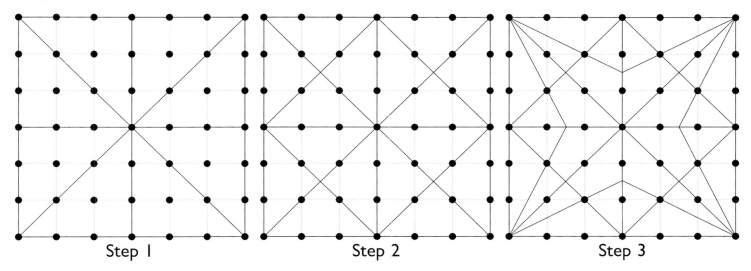

Step 1   Step 2   Step 3

1 Outline a 6 × 6 square on squared paper.
2 Using a sharp pencil and a ruler, copy steps 1, 2 and 3.
3 Colour your Islamic pattern to highlight its symmetry.
4 Repeat steps 1, 2 and 3 and make a different pattern.

Challenge

Make an Islamic pattern and, by repeating it four times, make a tiling design.

The example shows the construction lines and the emerging pattern.

You can copy this pattern or design one of your own.

Colour your Islamic tiling pattern.

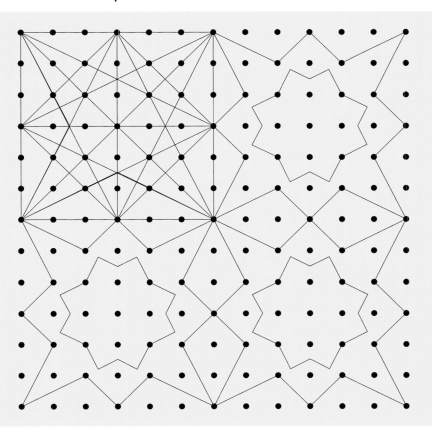

Puzzling pentominoes

Practice

A pentomino is a shape made from five identical squares touching edge to edge.
They can look like letters of the alphabet.

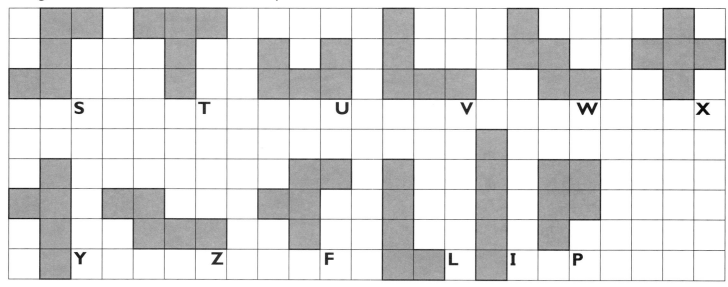

For each question, copy the shape on to squared paper and use two colours to show the different pentominoes.

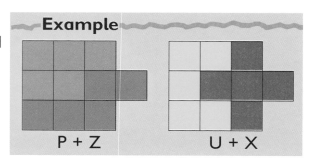

Example

P + Z   U + X

I Divide each shape into two pentominoes.

  a Do it two different ways for shape a.

  b Do it three different ways for shape b.

  c Find four different ways for shape c.

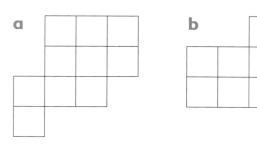

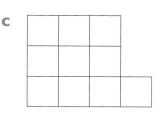

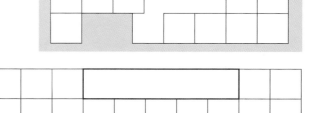

Refresher

1 Write the letter of the pentomino
   which will complete these rectangles.

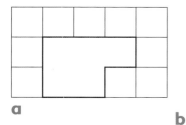

a

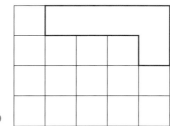

b

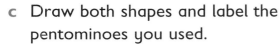
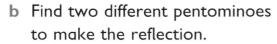

c

2 a Fit together the pentominoes
      S and W to make this shape.

   b Find two different pentominoes
      to make the reflection.

   c Draw both shapes and label the
      pentominoes you used.

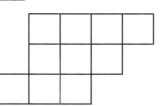

Challenge

This double-size T has 20 squares.
It is made with a set of four
pentominoes.

1 Make this double-size U using
   the pentominoes L, S, V and Z.
   Record on squared paper.
   Use colour to identify each
   pentomino.

Letter   Solution

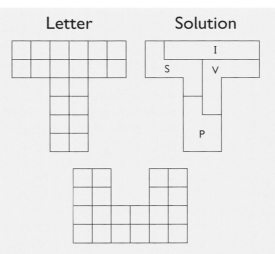

2 Using the four different pentominoes each time, make these double-size letters.
   Record them on squared paper. Colour the individual pentominoes in each shape.

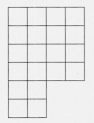
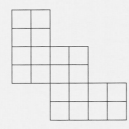
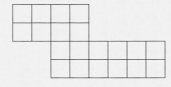

Translating patterns

Practice

1 Construct translation strip patterns on squared paper using these instructions for direction and distance.

2 Colour part of the pattern.

Example

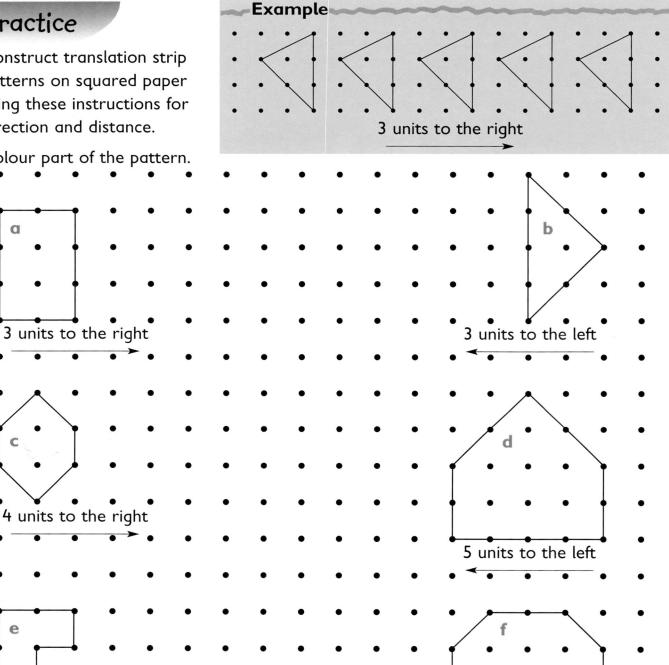

3 units to the right

a

3 units to the right

b

3 units to the left

c

4 units to the right

d

5 units to the left

e

2 units to the right

f

3 units to the left

3 a Design two translation patterns of your own.

b Draw an arrow and write the instructions below each pattern.

Refresher

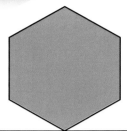 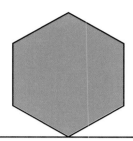 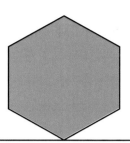

5 cm to the right

1 Follow these steps to make the sliding pattern.

- Rule a line 20 cm long.
- Mark points at 5 cm, 10 cm, 15 cm.
- Place the vertex of a hexagon at 5 cm and draw round the shape.
- Slide the shape along to 10 cm and draw round it.
- Repeat at the 15 cm mark.
- Label your sliding pattern.

2 Choose a different shape and repeat the above steps.

Challenge

You need:
- a sheet of squared paper or dot paper
- a plastic 2D shape
- colouring materials

Make three translating strip patterns with your shape.

In each pattern, the outline should overlap by a different amount.

Use an arrow to show the direction and the distance moved each time.

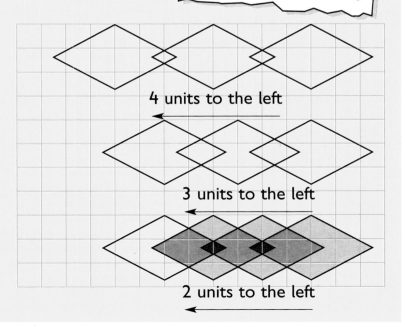

4 units to the left

3 units to the left

2 units to the left

Translating with co-ordinates

Practice

1   The co-ordinates of shape A are:
(0, 2), (0, 6), (2, 5), (2, 3).

   a   Add 3 units to the first number in A's
co-ordinates to make shape B.
Copy and complete:
(3, 2) (3, 6) (☐ , 5) (☐ , 3)
Plot the points and join them in order.

   b   Add 6 units to the first number in A's
co-ordinates to make shape C. Copy
and complete:
(6, 2) (☐ , 6) (☐ , ☐) (☐ , ☐)
Plot the points and join them in order.

   c   Copy and complete:
Shape A has been translated ☐ units
to the ☐ to make shape C.

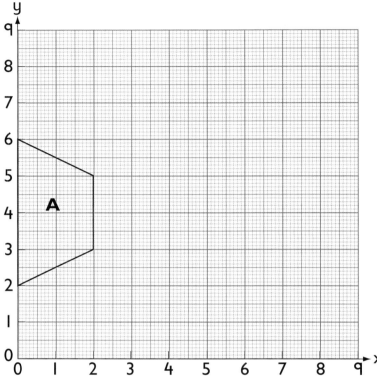

2   The co-ordinates of shape K are: (7, 5)
(9, 8) (9, 5) (8, 4).

   a   Subtract 3 units from the first number
in K's co-ordinates to make shape L.
Copy and complete:
(4, 5) (6, 8) (☐ , 5) (☐ , 4)
Plot the points and join them in order.

   b   Subtract 6 units from the first number
in K's co-ordinates to make shape M.
Copy and complete:
(1, 5) (☐ , ☐) (☐ , ☐) (☐ , ☐)
Plot the points and join them in order.

   c   Copy and complete:
Shape K has been translated ☐ units
to the ☐ make shape M.

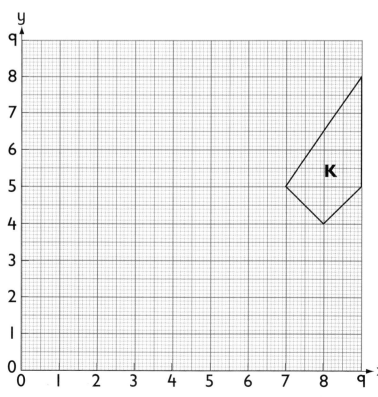

Refresher

1 Copy and complete the co-ordinates for:

Shape A: (1, 2) (1, 6) (3, ▢) (▢ , 2)

Shape B: (5, ▢) (▢ , 6) (▢ , ▢) (▢ , ▢)

Shape C: (9, ▢) (▢ , ▢) (▢ , ▢) (▢ , ▢)

2 Copy and complete:

Shape ▢ has been translated 8 units to the right to make shape ▢ .

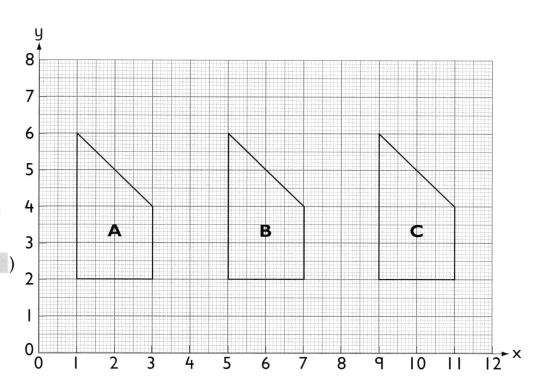

Challenge

1 The co-ordinates of shape A are:

(1, 4) (2, 5) (4, 4) (5, 2) (4, 1) (2, 2)

Add 3 units each time to the first co-ordinate of shape A.
Copy and complete:

Shape B (4, 4) (5, 5) (▢ , 4) (▢ , 2) (▢ , 1) (▢ , 2)

Shape C (7, 4) (8, 5) (▢ , 4) (▢ , 2) (▢ , 1) (▢ , 2)

Shape D (10, 4) (11, 5) (▢ , ▢) (▢ , ▢) (▢ , ▢) (▢ , ▢)

Plot these points on the grid and join them in order.

2 Add 3 units each time to the second co-ordinate of shape A.
Copy and complete:

Shape E (1, 7) (2, 8) (4, ▢) (2, ▢)

Shape F (1, 10) (2, 11) (▢ , ▢) (▢ , ▢) (▢ , ▢) (▢ , ▢)

The shape translates 3 units up each time.
Plot these points and join them in order.

3 Continue the translating pattern to the right and up until you have filled the grid.
Use two colours to show your repeating pattern.

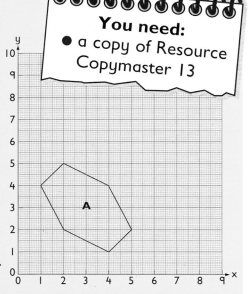

You need:
● a copy of Resource Copymaster 13

Tiling translations

Practice

1 a Copy these patterns on to 1 cm square dot paper.

   b Continue each pattern for four more large squares.

   c Colour a section of the pattern so that squares next to each other do not have the same colour. Use the least number of colours possible.

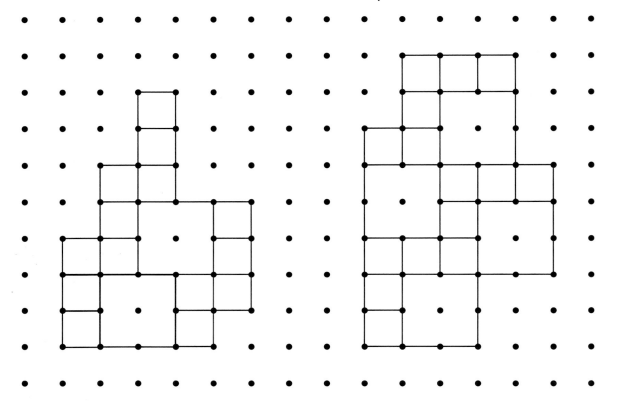

2 You need two sizes of equilateral triangles. Design your own pattern. Copy it on to 1 cm triangular dot paper. Colour part of your pattern.

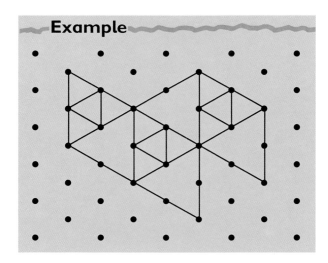

Example

Refresher

Work with a partner.

You need a supply of regular triangles and hexagons.

Make these patterns with your shapes.

a
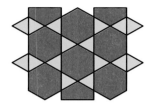

b
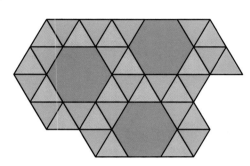

Challenge

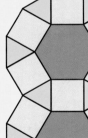

You need:
● a supply of regular polygons

Work with a partner.

1 Use triangles, squares and hexagons to make these translation patterns.

a
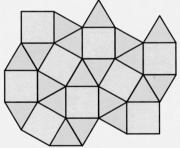

b

c

2 Use your regular polygons to make a different tiling translation.

Puzzle time

Practice

JUNE						
S	M	T	W	T	F	S
				1	2	3

1 Carole's birthday is on 24 June.
On which day of the week is it?

2 Henry VIII's wife Anne was Queen for 1000 days.
For how many years and days was she Queen?

3 **Longerlife Lighting Company**

Our light bulbs are guaranteed to last for 1000 hours.

You see the advert and buy a light bulb.
If the company's claim is true, for how many weeks, days and hours should the light bulb last?

4 Use the information to work out the ages of these children.

Jack: I am two years younger than Terry.

Jo: I am a year older than Jack.

Katie: I am three years younger than Terry.
          I will be 10 next year.

5 Rosie and Bruce are mother and son.

Bruce is now the same age that Rosie was four years ago.
Four years ago Bruce was half his mother's age.
Rosie is now 12 years old. What age is her son?

6 Make up a puzzle, like the one in question 5.
Ask a friend to solve it.

Refresher

This time machine tests for leap years.

Enter each year into the machine to find out whether or not it is a leap year.

a 2000
b 1990
c 2010
d 1900
e 2020
f 2400

Challenge

1 Ashrif was at a friend's birthday party on 20 March 2000.

"You're lucky," he said to his friend.
"I'm also 12 years old but I've only had 3 'proper' birthdays."

What is Ashrif's date of birth?

2 "That's nothing," replied his friend.
"My great, great uncle was 8 before he had his first 'proper' birthday."

What was the great, great uncle's date of birth?
Explain your reasoning.

83

Making connections

Practice

1 This is a bus timetable from Cambridge to Luton Airport. Buses leave every two hours.

Cambridge	11:00	13:00	15:00	17:00
Trumpington	11:10	13:10		
Harston	11:15	13:15		
Royston	11:25	13:25		
Baldock	11:40			
Letchworth	11:42			
Hitchin	11:50			
Luton Airport	12:05	14:05	16:05	18:05

  a Copy and complete the bus timetable.
  b How long is the bus journey from Cambridge to Luton Airport?
  c You have to arrive at the airport at 5 minutes past 4 p.m. Which bus would you catch at Baldock?
  d The 17:00 bus is 17 minutes late at Royston. At what time does it arrive?

2 This table shows some of the train times from Kings Cross to Luton Airport.

Kings Cross	16:01	16:16	16:19	16:34	16:46	17:04
Luton Airport	16:31	16:46	17:02	17:04	17:16	17:37

  a The Express train takes exactly 30 minutes for the journey.
    Which of the above times from Kings Cross are for Express trains?
  b If you catch the 16:19 train, how long is the journey to Luton Airport in minutes?
  c At what time does the slowest train leave Kings Cross?
  d Your holiday flight departs from Luton Airport at 19:35.
    You need to allow 15 minutes for the bus shuttle from the station to the airport.
    You must check in two hours before departure.
    Which train should you catch at Kings Cross?

Refresher

This is the winter timetable for Friday flights between London Heathrow and Glasgow.
The flight takes 1 hour and 15 minutes.

a Copy and complete the timetable.
b The 10:55 flight is delayed by 20 minutes. At what time will it leave London?
c What is the new arrival time in Glasgow?

Depart London	Arrive Glasgow
07:05	
09:00	10:15
10: 55	
	14:10
15:30	
	18:15
19:15	
	23:00

Challenge

Your Gran is planning a holiday to Palma.

She is having difficulty in reading the timetable. (She blames it on her glasses!)

She wants to fly to Palma on a Saturday in June and return home on a Sunday flight two weeks later.

She wants to fly during daytime and likes a window seat.

Look at the timetable. Decide which is the best outward and return flight.
Write them in the 12-hour clock (Gran gets confused by the 24-hour clock).

Day	Luton to Palma			Palma to Luton		
	Flt. no.	Dep.	Arr.	Flt. no.	Dep.	Arr.
Mon–Fri	401	12:35	16:00	402	16:50	18:20
Mon–Fri	419	21:40	01:05	418*	01:45	03:15
Sat	407	10:40	14:05	406	14:45	16:15
Sat	401	12:35	16:00	402	16:50	18:20
Sat	409	17:05	20:30	408	21:10	22:40
Sat	421	21:15	00:40			
Sun				424	01:20	02:50
Sun	413	06:20	09:45	412	10:25	11:55
Sun	401	12:35	16:00	402	16:50	18:20
*Except Monday						

Measuring capacities

Practice

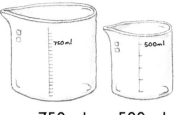 

750 ml   500 ml   250 ml   100 ml   50 ml

1 You have these measuring cylinders and an empty container.

   a Write five ways to pour 1 litre of water into the container using:

   2 measures

   3 measures

   4 measures

   5 measures

   Example
   1 litre = 500 ml + 250 ml + 250 ml

   b Write three ways to pour $\frac{1}{2}$ litre of water into the container using:

   2 measures $\frac{1}{2}l = 250$ ml + ?

   4 measures $\frac{1}{2}l = 100$ ml + ?

   6 measures $\frac{1}{2}l = 50$ ml + ?

2 You have three measuring jars and an empty container.

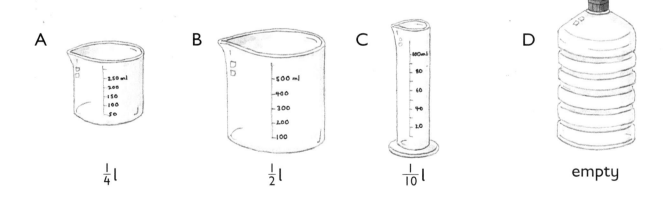

A $\frac{1}{4}l$ B $\frac{1}{2}l$ C $\frac{1}{10}l$ D   empty

The table below shows the amounts of water poured into an empty container D.
Work out how many millilitres of water container D held each day.

Monday	2 of A + 3 of B + 1 of C
Tuesday	4 of A + 1 of B + 2 of C
Wednesday	3 of A + 1 of B + 5 of C
Thursday	2 of A + 4 of B + 6 of C
Friday	5 of A + 4 of B + 3 of C

Refresher

1 Write these capacities in millilitres.

a $2\frac{1}{2}l$ b $3\frac{1}{4}l$

c $4\frac{3}{4}l$ d $7\frac{1}{10}l$

e $5\frac{1}{4}l$ f $6\frac{3}{4}l$

g $7\frac{1}{2}l$ h $1\frac{1}{10}l$

2 Write these capacities in litres and millilitres.

a 6250 ml   b 8410 ml

c 6200 ml   d 8400 ml

e 6050 ml   f 8010 ml

g 6020 ml   h 8040 ml

Challenge

mango 500 ml   pineapple 250 ml   lemon 100 ml   lime 50 ml   1 litre

1 You pour two or more of these measured amounts of fruit juice into an empty one litre jug. Show that you can make 10 different mixed fruit drinks.

2 You top up the jug to the one litre mark with orange juice.
How many millilitres of orange juice do you add each time?

87

Measuring millilitres

Practice

1 200 ml more water is poured into each measuring jar.
   Write the new water level.

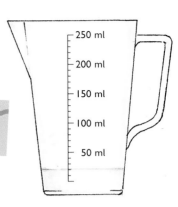

Example
20 ml + 200 ml = 220 ml

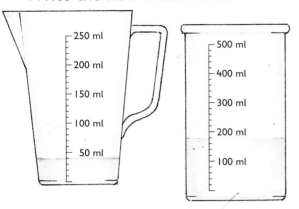

2 150 ml of water is poured out of each container.
   Work out how many millilitres of water are left in each.

a
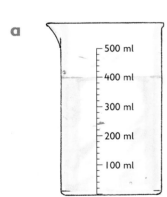

b
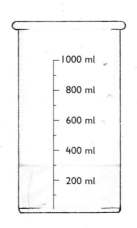

c
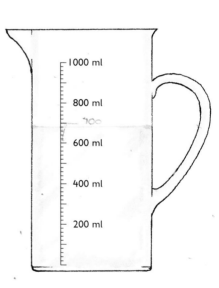

3 Pour water into each jar to raise the level to 1 litre.
   Write how many millilitres you add to each jar.

a
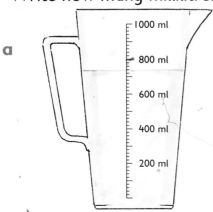

b

c

Refresher

Each pair of jars shows the level before and after some water was added.
Write how many millilitres of water is poured into the jar each time.

Example

before 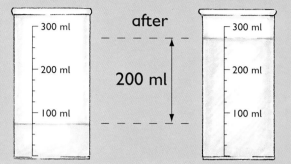 after

200 ml

a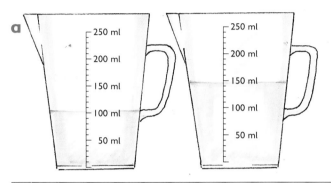

b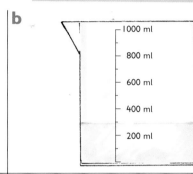

c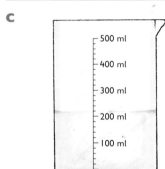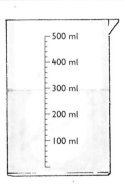

d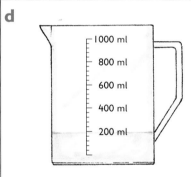

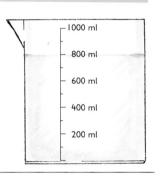

Challenge

Find a way to measure the amount of vinegar which is added to a jar of pickled onions.
Use marbles for onions and water for vinegar.

Remember

Leave about 1 cm of space at the top of the jar.

Your group needs:
- a clear, uncalibrated plastic bottle or jar (with lid if possible)
- marbles
- funnel
- water
- measuring cylinder

89

Picnic litres

Practice

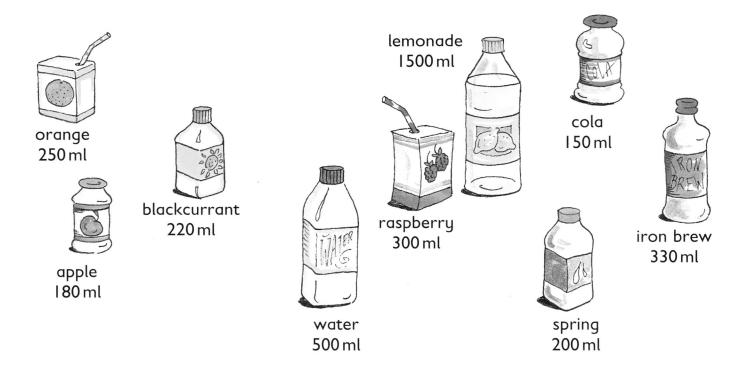

orange
250 ml

apple
180 ml

blackcurrant
220 ml

water
500 ml

lemonade
1500 ml

raspberry
300 ml

cola
150 ml

spring
200 ml

iron brew
330 ml

Some children bought these drinks for the class outing.

1 Change each capacity from millilitres to litres.
   Record in decimal form.
   Total the capacities. Write the answer in decimal form.

Example	
apple	180 ml = 0·18 l
water	500 ml = 0·5 l
	680 ml = 0·68 l

a Andy   orange 250 ml
            water 500 ml

b Beth   blackcurrant 220 ml
            raspberry 300 ml

c Carol   apple 180 ml
            spring 200 ml

d David   lemonade 1500 ml
            cola 150 ml

e Ewan   orange 250 ml
            apple 180 ml

f Fiona   apple 180 ml
            iron brew 330 ml

2 Find two soft drinks which make these total capacities:

   a 2·0 l   b 0·42 l   c 1·83 l   d 0·58 l

3 Find the total capacity of two cans of iron brew and two bottles of lemonade.

Refresher

Write the pairs of capacities that are the same.
Then find the "odd one out".

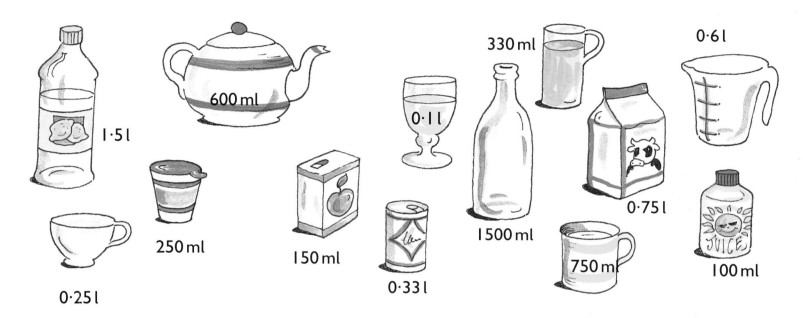

1·5 l

600 ml

0·1 l

330 ml

0·6 l

250 ml

150 ml

1500 ml

0·75 l

750 ml

100 ml

0·25 l

0·33 l

Challenge

Work in a small group.

Find a way to measure the capacity
of your drinking straw.

You need:
- a drinking straw each
- water
- measuring jar
- beaker
- a paper towel

Hint:
You may find some
Blu-tack or Plasticine
helpful.

91

Pints and gallons

Practice

1 You have one each of these glasses and a pint of milk.

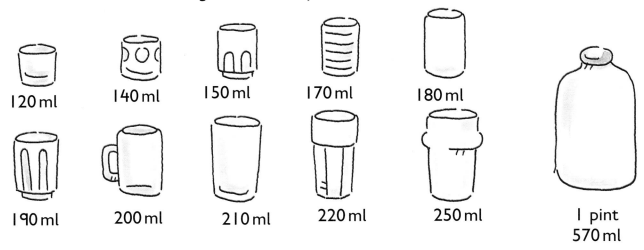

120 ml 140 ml 150 ml 170 ml 180 ml

190 ml 200 ml 210 ml 220 ml 250 ml 1 pint 570 ml

Work out how to pour the milk to fill three glasses exactly with no milk left in the bottle.
Find as many different ways as you can.
How do I rate?

Example
170 ml + 180 ml + 220 ml = 570 ml

Score	
4 ways	☆
5–6 ways	☆☆☆
More than 6 ways	☆☆☆☆☆

2 You fill all the glasses in question 1 with milk.

   a How many litres of milk do the 10 glasses hold altogether?

   b How many pint bottles of milk will you need to fill the glasses?

3 Jean found this advert in an old magazine. The slogan said that children should:

Drink a pinta milk a day.

She used the relationship: 1 pint = 570 ml and did some calculating.
What was her answer to the amount of milk she should drink in one week:

   a in millilitres?

   b in litres?

92

Refresher

In the United States, liquids are measured in pints and gallons.

A pint is slightly more than $\frac{1}{2}$ litre.

1 pint is approximately equal to 570 ml.

A gallon is a bit less than 5 litres.

1 Write **true** or **false** for each of these statements.

  a 1 pint > 500 ml   b 1 pint > $\frac{1}{2}$ litre

  c 1 litre < 1 pint   d 1 pint < 1 litre

  e 1000 ml > 1 pint   f 0·5 l > 1 pint

  g 570 ml < $\frac{1}{2}$ litre   h 0·5 l < 570 ml

2 Write the correct sign, < or >, to make these sentences **true**.

  a 5 litres   1 gallon   b 1 gallon   5 litres

  c 2 gallons   10 litres   d 3 gallons   10 litres

Challenge

Type of car	Miles per gallon (mpg)
A Hatchback	48
B Saloon	40
C Estate	36
D 4 × 4	20

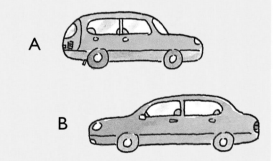

1 Cars B and D each make a journey of 100 miles.

  a How many gallons of petrol will each car use
     to travel 100 miles?

  b Approximately how many litres of petrol will
     each car use for the journey?

2 Cars A and C each make a round trip of
   144 miles. Approximately how many litres of
   petrol will each car use?

Banquet litres

Practice

1 The cook has prepared 40 litres of chicken soup for the starter course.
Each soup plate is 250 ml.

   a How many guests can have a plate of soup?

   b Only 120 guests take the soup. How many litres of soup are
left over for the kitchen staff?

2 The recipe for tomato sauce is:
5 tomatoes make 500 ml of sauce.

   a How much sauce can the kitchen boy make with 25 tomatoes?

   b The cook orders him to make 5 litres of sauce. How many
tomatoes will he need?

3 The copper cauldron holds 60 litres of hot water.
The brass urn holds $2\frac{1}{2}$ times as much.

   a How many litres does the brass urn hold?

   b The scullery maid uses 18 litres of hot water from the urn to wash
dishes. How many litres of water does the urn now hold?

4 The pantry maid is filling the butter churn with milk.
A full churn holds 7·5 litres.
A full jug holds 500 ml.

   a How many jugs of milk will fill the churn?

5 Look at the pots in the Refresher section.
The assistant cook uses pots d and e to boil vegetables.
What is the total capacity of the pots?

Refresher

In the Elizabethan kitchen of Burghley House, Stamford, the copper pots and saucepans are hung in a row.

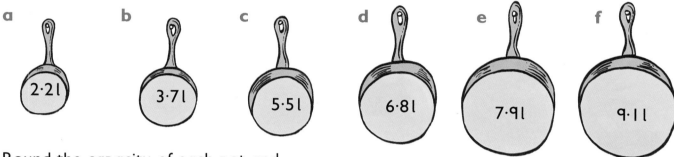

a   2·2l   b   3·7l   c   5·5l   d   6·8l   e   7·9l   f   9·1l

Round the capacity of each pot and saucepan to the nearest litre.

Example

4·6l = 5l to nearest litre

Challenge

These old storage jars all contain some olive oil.
The amount in each higher jar is the sum of the two jars below.

1 How many litres of olive oil are in the top jar?

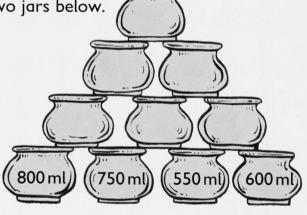

800 ml   750 ml   550 ml   600 ml

2 These bottom row jars can go in any order.
How many top jar capacities can you have by arranging the bottom row of jars in different ways?

700 ml   650 ml   750 ml   500 ml

Adding and subtracting in your head

Practice

1 Work out the first calculation and use it to help you work out the other two.

a 2 + 5 + 8 + 3
   20 + 50 + 80 + 30
   200 + 500 + 800 + 300

e 800 + 100 + 300 + 500
   8 + 1 + 3 + 5
   80 + 10 + 30 + 50

b 6 + 7 + 2 + 4
   60 + 70 + 20 + 40
   600 + 700 + 200 + 400

f 9 + 4 + 7 + 5 + 6
   900 + 400 + 700 + 500 + 600
   90 + 40 + 70 + 50 + 60

c 80 + 10 + 90 + 50
   8 + 1 + 9 + 5
   800 + 100 + 900 + 500

g 30 + 40 + 80 + 60 + 90
   3 + 4 + 8 + 6 + 9
   300 + 400 + 800 + 600 + 900

d 600 + 400 + 700 + 300
   60 + 40 + 70 + 30
   6 + 4 + 7 + 3

h 700 + 800 + 400 + 500 + 200
   70 + 80 + 40 + 50 + 20
   7 + 8 + 4 + 5 + 2

2 Work out these calculations in your head.

a 570 + 240
   360 + 410
   250 + 470
   810 + 360
   460 + 320

d 1263 − 500
   1432 − 800
   1025 − 300
   1487 − 600
   1356 − 700

b 850 − 630
   750 − 420
   340 − 180
   980 − 490
   670 − 520

e 230 + 364
   458 + 340
   384 + 380
   410 + 269
   746 + 220

c 638 + 500
   742 + 600
   389 + 900
   476 + 600
   861 + 500

f 584 − 340
   496 − 230
   754 − 560
   672 − 490
   820 − 342

3 Now choose one calculation from each section and explain how you worked it out.
   You can use numbers or words.

Refresher

Work out the calculations. Use your number facts to help yo

a 6 + 4 + 3
   60 + 40 + 30
   600 + 400 + 300

b 2 + 4 + 1
   20 + 40 + 10
   200 + 400 + 100

c 5 + 3 + 1
   50 + 30 + 10
   500 + 300 + 100

d 6 + 7 + 5
   60 + 70 + 50
   600 + 700 + 500

e 9 + 3 + 2
   90 + 30 + 20
   900 + 300 + 200

f 130 + 150
   240 + 210
   270 + 310
   330 + 240
   560 + 330

g 350 − 240
   480 − 350
   450 − 220
   380 − 270
   550 − 340

h 120 + 235
   320 + 245
   450 + 338
   247 + 330
   561 + 130

Challenge

Write 1500 in the middle of your page. Think of as many addition or subtraction calculations where the answer is 1500. Make them as different as possible.

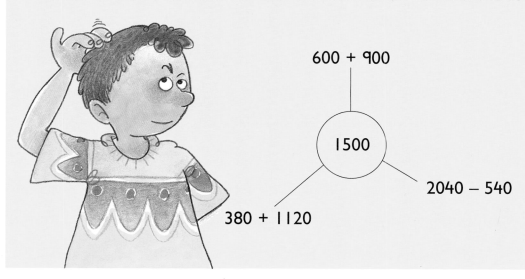

600 + 900

1500

2040 − 540

380 + 1120

● Derive quickly or continue to derive quickly all two digit pairs that total 100
● Use known facts and place value for mental addition and subtraction
● Derive quickly or continue to derive quickly decimals that total 1

Adding and subtracting in your head again

Practice

Work out the calculations in your head.

1 a 428 + ☐ = 500   f 435 + ☐ = 500
   b 651 + ☐ = 700   g 751 + ☐ = 800
   c 168 + ☐ = 200   h 816 + ☐ = 900
   d 546 + ☐ = 600   i 529 + ☐ = 600
   e 873 + ☐ = 900   j 982 + ☐ = 1000

2 a 4·8 + ☐ = 5   f 3·2 + ☐ = 4
   b 3·7 + ☐ = 4   g 9·3 + ☐ = 10
   c 8·1 + ☐ = 9   h 1·5 + ☐ = 2
   d 4·6 + ☐ = 5   i 7·9 + ☐ = 8
   e 5·7 + ☐ = 6   j 8·4 + ☐ = 9

3 a 5·7 + 2·5 = ☐   f 8·3 + 1·9 = ☐
   b 4·6 + 3·8 = ☐   g 7·8 + 2·4 = ☐
   c 2·7 + 3·9 = ☐   h 6·5 + 7·7 = ☐
   d 3·5 + 5·6 = ☐   i 3·6 + 4·6 = ☐
   e 4·2 + 6·8 = ☐   j 7·1 + 5·9 = ☐

4 a 6·2 − 3·8 = ☐   f 6·1 − 3·5 = ☐
   b 4·5 − 2·7 = ☐   g 6·2 − 2·7 = ☐
   c 3·4 − 2·7 = ☐   h 9·2 − 5·4 = ☐
   d 6·8 − 5·9 = ☐   i 8·1 − 3·6 = ☐
   e 7·4 − 3·8 = ☐   j 7·2 − 5·4 = ☐

5 a 0·26 + 0·54 = ☐   f 0·47 + 0·69 = ☐
   b 0·85 + 0·47 = ☐   g 0·99 + 0·21 = ☐
   c 0·61 + 0·39 = ☐   h 0·61 + 0·37 = ☐
   d 0·78 + 0·51 = ☐   i 0·48 + 0·73 = ☐
   e 0·33 + 0·84 = ☐   j 0·86 + 0·49 = ☐

6 Now choose one calculation from each section and explain how you worked it out.

Refresher

1 Work out the calculations in your head.
Use the answer to the first calculation to help you work out the second.

a 28 + [ ] = 100   328 + [ ] = 400   f 29 + [ ] = 100   529 + [ ] = 600
b 52 + [ ] =100   452 + [ ] = 500   g 38 + [ ] = 100   438 + [ ] = 500
c 34 + [ ] = 100   734 + [ ] = 800   h 55 + [ ] = 100   655 + [ ] = 700
d 81 + [ ] = 100   681 + [ ] = 700   i 42 + [ ] = 100   742 + [ ] = 800
e 67 + [ ] = 100   267 + [ ] = 300   j 73 + [ ] = 100   873 + [ ] = 900

2 Work out what goes with the decimal to equal the next whole number.
Use the answer to the first calculation to help you work out the second.

a 0·8 + [ ] = 1   2·8 + [ ] = 3   e 0·3 + [ ] = 1   5·3 + [ ] = 6
b 0·4 + [ ] = 1   2·4 + [ ] = 3   f 0·7 + [ ] = 1   1·7 + [ ] = 2
c 0·2 + [ ] = 1   3·2 + [ ] = 4   g 0·6 + [ ] = 1   5·6 + [ ] = 6
d 0·1 + [ ] = 1   4·1 + [ ] = 5   h 0·5 + [ ] = 1   7·5 + [ ] = 8

3 Add and subtract the decimals.

a 2·3 + 1·4 = [ ]   f 5·6 − 2·3 = [ ]
b 1·5 + 1·2 = [ ]   g 4·8 − 3·5 = [ ]
c 2·6 + 2·1 = [ ]   h 4·6 − 1·3 = [ ]
d 3·3 + 3·5 = [ ]   i 5·9 − 4·1 = [ ]
e 3·7 + 2·1 = [ ]   j 6·8 − 2·7 = [ ]

Challenge

Write 7·4 in the middle of your page. Think of as many addition or subtraction calculations where the answer is 7·4. Make them as different as possible.

3·6 + 3·8

(7·4)

10·7 − 3·3

99

Adding using the written way

Practice

1 Write these calculations out vertically and then work out the answers.
Be sure to write the digits in the correct columns.

a 6832 + 149
b 4136 + 793
c 5872 + 516
d 4341 + 467
e 5107 + 738
f 3263 + 654
g 5125 + 907
h 6254 + 389
i 8834 + 207
j 4468 + 645
k 8045 + 579
l 9324 + 858

2 Now calculate these.

a £26·84 + £13·52
b £17·62 + £21·52
c £53·41 + £37·24
d £52·12 + £29·38
e £37·86 + £15·61
f £49·72 + £23·18

3 Work out these.

a 4·32 m + 5·75 m
b 5·82 cm + 2·40 cm
c 6·72 kg + 6·19 kg
d 6·72 km + 2·59 km
e 8·65 km + 5·27 km
f 7·95 m + 2·62 m

Refresher

1 Now work these out.

a 482 + 234

b 345 + 527

c 227 + 354

d 652 + 274

e 437 + 246

f 728 + 237

g 259 + 690

h 407 + 239

i 565 + 305

j 724 + 138

Example

```
  | 5 | 6 | 3 |
+ | 2 | 6 | 4 |
  | 8 | 2 | 7 |
      | 1 |
```

Don't forget to line up the decimal points.

2 Can you calculate these?

a £16·72 + £20·26

b £15·81 + £42·07

c £24·21 + £35·65

d £34·28 + £25·31

e £48·61 + £50·37

Example

£16·72
+ £20·26
£36·98

3 Give the answers to these.

a 5·83 m + 3·14 m

b 6·42 kg + 2·39 kg

c 9·72 cm + 2·06 cm

d 4·89 m + 5·05 m

e 5·72 km + 3·75 km

Challenge

1 Look at all the calculations in the Practice section. Investigate the pattern of adding odd and even numbers. How could you use this pattern to check your results?

Odd + odd = ?

Odd + even = ?

Even + even = ?

2 What happens if more than two numbers are added?

Subtracting using the written way

Practice

1 Write these calculations out vertically and then work out the answers.
Be sure to write the digits in the correct columns.

a 5862 − 35
b 7435 − 908
c 4920 − 751
d 6137 − 408
e 8492 − 378
f 5024 − 617
g 8154 − 827
h 9264 − 539
i 6748 − 689
j 8246 − 528
k 7594 − 835
l 4761 − 872

2 Can you calculate these?

a £46·12 − £37·08
b £37·41 − £28·27
c £47·26 − £19·07
d £54·35 − £27·51
e £65·74 − £31·85
f £91·58 − £39·09

3 Give the answers to these.

a 8·94 m − 3·27 m
b 12·73 cm − 8·55 cm
c 15·04 kg − 7·32 kg
d 9·27 km − 6·82 km
e 17·83 km − 9·26 km
f 18·63 m − 9·07 m

Refresher

1 Give the answers to these.

a 947 − 319
b 862 − 435
c 725 − 362
d 605 − 241
e 513 − 272
f 468 − 129
g 806 − 534
h 937 − 308
i 572 − 237
j 824 − 458

2 Now calculate these.

a 8·72 km − 3·21 km
b 6·86 m − 2·72 m
c 7·15 kg − 3·58 kg
d 9·62 m − 5·18 m
e 8·12 km − 3·40 km
f 7·67 m − 2·19 m

Challenge

Change these measures to the same unit and then subtract them.

a 8·25 km − 750 m
b 7·47 kg − 483 g
c 6·51 m − 189 cm
d 15·73 km − 847 m
e 24·67 kg − 627 g

Solve the problems

Practice

You can work out these problems in your head, in your head but with jottings, with a calculator or using the vertical methods.

Work out the answers to the problems. Choose the method you are going to use. Explain **why** you choose that method.

a I went out with £21·72 and came home with £3·52. I bought a book for £5·49 and spent the rest on a T-shirt. How much was the T-shirt?

b The school has ordered 1400 new pens, 300 red, 600 blue and the rest black. How many black pens have been ordered?

c I counted how many hours of sleep I have had in the last three nights. The total is 24 hours sleep. One night I slept for 9 hours, and 7 the next. How many hours did I sleep on the third night?

d In three very busy days 1487 people visited an art gallery. 596 came one day, 682 the next. How many came on the third day?

e I measured the length of the playground. The total length was 67·41 m. The grassy area was 19·54 m, the quiet area was 8·13 m. How long was the rest?

Refresher

Work out the answers to the problems. Choose the method you are going to use. Explain **why** you chose that method.

a I counted the number of pencils on each table. There were seven on one table, six on another, and eight on the other two tables. How many pencils altogether?

b I have been swimming three times this week. On Monday I swam 400 m, on Wednesday 300 m and on Friday 500 m. What was the total number of metres I swam?

c I want to buy a new shirt for £28·76. I have £14·32 so far. How much more do I need?

d On sports day the school made £42·56 from selling cold drinks and £38·23 from selling cakes. How much money was made altogether?

Challenge

Work out the answer to this problem in your head.

Four girls competed in the long jump on sports day. Helen, who is 9 years old, jumped 5 cm further than Grace. Grace jumped 2 cm less than Rosa, but 2 cm further than Molly. Molly and Grace are cousins.

If Rosa jumped 93 cm how far did the other three girls jump?

Finding factors

Practice

The spaceships have come to collect the aliens.
All aliens must be a factor of the number on the spaceship.
Aliens must board the spaceship in pairs.
Find the aliens that are factors and give them a partner.

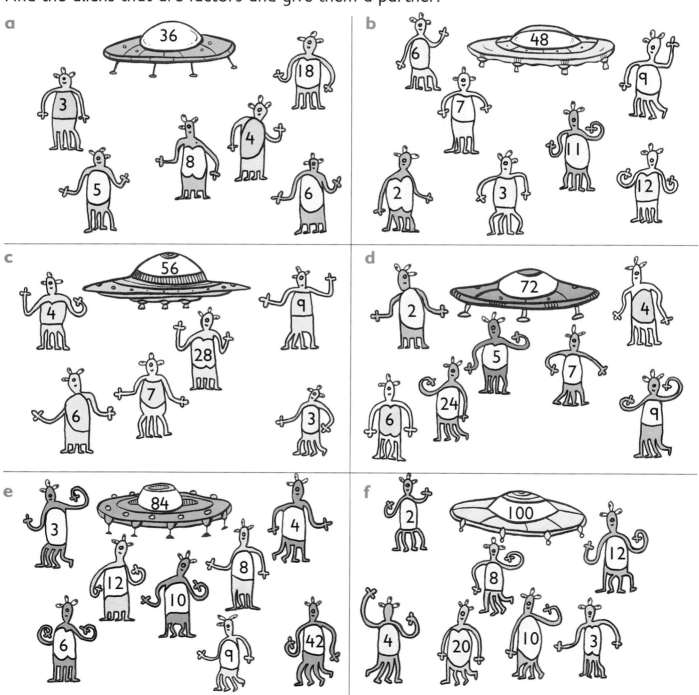

a

b

c

d

e

f

Refresher

1 Write two multiplication number sentences for each set of numbers.
Decide which numbers are the factors and which number is the product.

> **Example**
> $4 \times 3 = 12$
> $3 \times 4 = 12$

a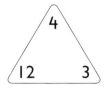
4
12   3

b
6   4
24

c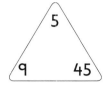
5
9   45

d
21   3
7

e
9
8   56

f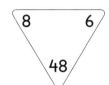
8   6
48

g
70
7   10

h
2   12
24

i
7
9   63

j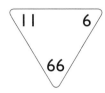
11   6
66

2 Find the missing factor or product. Write a multiplication number sentence.

a
5
11

b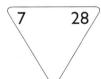
7   28

c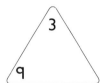
3
9

d
4   32

e
6
54

Challenge

Try these.

a Which number is always a factor of any number? Why?

b There are six factors of 32. What are they? Find two other numbers greater than 20 with exactly six factors.

c A number has the factors 2, 3, 5 and 7. What number could it be? Find three other factors.

d How many different ways can a class of 30 children be split into equal teams? What about a class of 26 children? 28 children?

e If the number of children in the class increases, will there be more ways to split the class into equal size teams? Explain.

Finding common factors

Practice

1 Write all of the factors for each pair of numbers in order.
Circle the common factors for each pair.

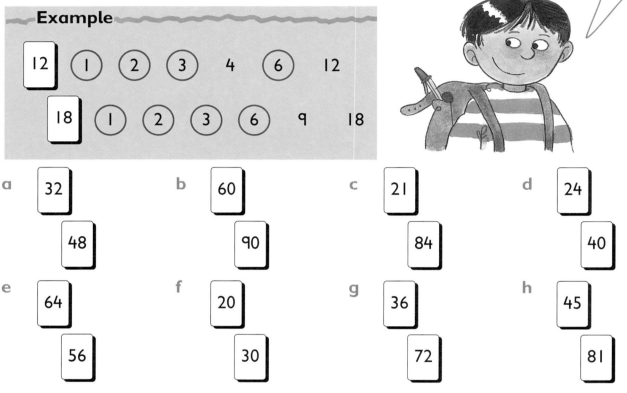

Example

12 | ① ② ③ 4 ⑥ 12

18 | ① ② ③ ⑥ 9 18

a 32 / 48

b 60 / 90

c 21 / 84

d 24 / 40

e 64 / 56

f 20 / 30

g 36 / 72

h 45 / 81

2 Write all of the factors for each set of three numbers in order.
Circle the **highest common factor**.

Example

12 | 1 2 ③ 4 6 12

18 | 1 2 ③ 6 9 18

21 | 1 ③ 7 21

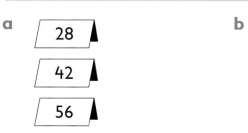

a 28 / 42 / 56

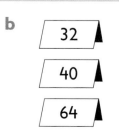

b 32 / 40 / 64

c 50 / 75 / 100

Refresher

Fill in the missing factors.
Copy and complete.

a   ☐ × 3 = 21   f   ☐ × 12 = 48

b   4 × ☐ = 28   g   ☐ × 2 = 18

c   7 × ☐ = 49   h   5 × ☐ = 25

d   6 × ☐ = 48   i   ☐ × 8 = 56

e   ☐ × 9 = 45   j   6 × ☐ = 54

2 Fill in the missing products.
   Copy and complete.

a   8 × 8 = ☐   f   4 × 20 = ☐

b   4 × 9 = ☐   g   2 × 25 = ☐

c   8 × 11 = ☐   h   9 × 9 = ☐

d   2 × 28 = ☐   i   4 × 15 = ☐

e   3 × 13 = ☐   j   12 × 6 = ☐

Challenge

Try these.

a All of the common factors of 75 and 100 except 1 are multiples of the same
   number. What is the number?

b If 3 is not a common factor of a pair of numbers, what other numbers can't be
   common factors? Explain why.

c Some even numbers have only even factors except for 1.
   Others have odd factors also.
   Find five others of each type.
   What do you notice?

Example
16 → 1, 2, 4, 8, 16
10 → 1, 2, 5, 10

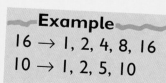

d Find three pairs of numbers where the second one is double the first one and has
   twice as many factors as the first one.

Finding out about odd and even numbers

Practice

Use the numbers shown to complete these statements.

Try at least five examples before making a general statement.

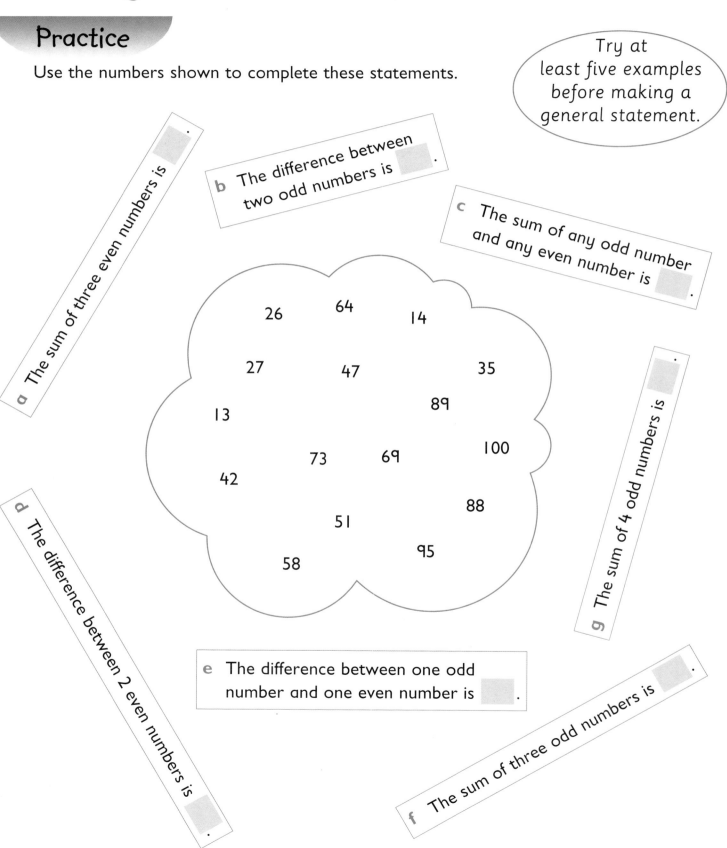

a The sum of three even numbers is ▢.

b The difference between two odd numbers is ▢.

c The sum of any odd number and any even number is ▢.

26   64   14

27   47   35

13   89

73   69   100

42

88

51

58   95

d The difference between 2 even numbers is ▢.

e The difference between one odd number and one even number is ▢.

f The sum of three odd numbers is ▢.

g The sum of 4 odd numbers is ▢.

Refresher

1 Copy and complete each table by finding numbers that fit.

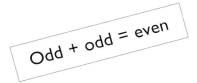

a Even

+	4		
6	10		

(Even)

b Odd

+			

(Odd)

c Odd

+			

(Even)

2 Match each statement below with the correct table.

Odd + odd = even

Even + even = even

Odd + even = odd

Challenge

Write your own statements for these.
Try out other examples to match your statement.
Is your statement correct?

Words to think about: product, sum, consecutive, odd, even

a $6 \times 9 = 54$

b 26 + 27 = 53

c $11 \times 12 = 132$

d $13 \times 9 = 117$

f $8 \times 12 = 96$

e $3 \times 5 \times 7 = 105$

g 26 + 32 + 14 + 40 = 112

Number sequences

Practice

Identify the rule.

1 Write the next five numbers in each sequence and then write the rule.

a 514, 520, 526, ▭ , ▭ , ▭ , ▭ , ▭   The rule is

b 2, 20, 200, ▭ , ▭ , ▭ , ▭ , ▭   The rule is

c 1→3→6→10→ ▭ → ▭ → ▭ → ▭ → ▭   The rule is

d 3 ⟍ 6 ⟋ 8 ⟍ 11 ⟋ ▭ ⟍ ▭ ⟋ ▭ ⟍ ▭   The rule is

e 2→4→6→10→ ▭ → ▭ → ▭ → ▭   The rule is

f 298→287→276→ ▭ → ▭ → ▭ → ▭ → ▭   The rule is

g −48, −42, −36, ▭ , ▭ , ▭ , ▭ , ▭   The rule is

h 4 ⟍ 40 ⟋ 20 ⟍ 200 ⟋ 100 ⟍ ▭ ⟋ ▭ ⟍ ▭ ⟋ ▭   The rule is

2 The rule for this number sequence is "double and subtract 1".
   Write the missing numbers to complete each sequence.

a 2 → 3 → 5 → 9 → ▭   b ▭ → 13 → 25 → 49

c 12 → ▭ → ▭ → 89 → 177   d 10 → 19 → 37 → ▭ → ▭

3 The rule is to add the same number each time.
   Write the missing numbers to complete the sequences.

a | 2 | | | | 18 |

c | 50 | | | | 150 |

b | 10 | | | | 58 |

d | 3 | | | | 407 |

Refresher

Write the next 10 numbers in each of these numbers sequences using the rule shown.

a (The rule is add 3 each time)

336 _ 339 _ [ ] [ ] [ ] [ ] [ ] [ ] [ ] [ ]
+3   +3   +3

b (The rule is subtract 5 each time.)

625 _ 620 _ [ ] [ ] [ ] [ ] [ ] [ ] [ ] [ ]
−5   −5

c (The rule is add 11 each time.)

99 _ −88 _ [ ] [ ] [ ] [ ] [ ] [ ] [ ] [ ]
+11   +11

d (The rule is halve each time.)

10 240 5120 _ [ ] [ ] [ ] [ ] [ ] [ ] [ ] [ ]
÷2   ÷2

e (The rule is multiply by 2 each time.)

3 _ 6 _ [ ] [ ] [ ] [ ] [ ] [ ] [ ] [ ]
×2   ×2

f (The rule is add the two previous numbers.)

1 _ 2 _ 3 _ 5 [ ] [ ] [ ] [ ] [ ] [ ] [ ] [ ]
1 + 2   2 + 3   3 + 5

Challenge

1 Write the type of number sequence for each example in question 1 on the Practice page.

2 Construct two number sequences of your own for each type of number sequence shown.

3 Rewrite your sequences on a separate piece of paper, deleting some of the numbers. Give the sequences to a friend to complete.

Types of number sequence

Add or subtract the same number each time.

Multiply or divide the same number each time.

Add or subtract a changing number.

Add the previous two numbers.

Combine two operations.

Number patterns

Practice

Look at each of the patterns below.

- Draw the next 3 patterns for each sequence.
- Write an addition number sentence for each.
- Identify and write the rule for extending each sequence.
- Write how many shapes will be in the tenth and twelfth pattern.

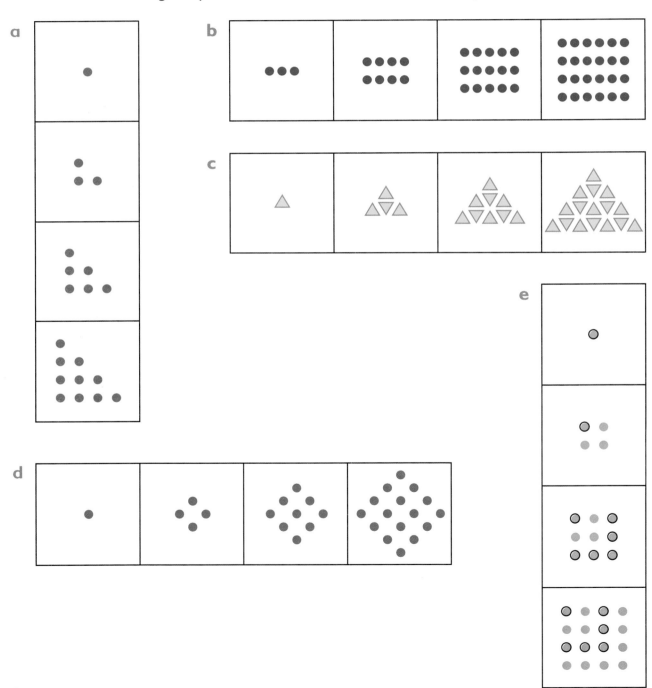

Refresher

Look at the pattern below.

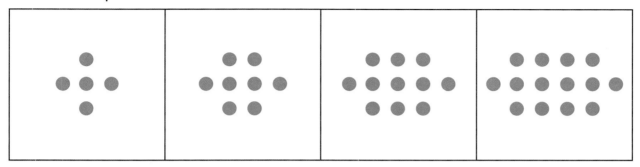

a   Count the number of dots in each sequence.

b   Turn the dot sequence into a number sequence and write the number sequence.

c   What is the rule?

2   Look at the pattern below.

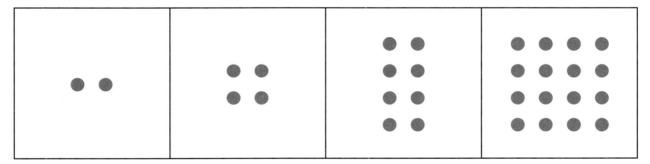

a   Count the number of dots in each sequence.

b   Turn the dot sequence into a number sequence and write the number sequence.

c   What is the rule?

Challenge

1   Make your own number patterns.

2   Start with one, two or three shapes. ○   △△   □□□

3   Draw the first four patterns for each sequence.

4   Swap patterns with a friend.

5   Complete the next three patterns of each sequence.

6   Work out the rule for each sequence.

Glossary

approximate

Approximate means *nearly* or *round about*. The sign ≈ means *is approximately equal to.*

See also estimate

angles

right angle

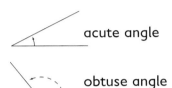

acute angle

obtuse angle

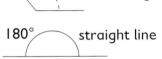

180° straight line

Angles are formed when two straight lines meet. We measure an **angle** by measuring the amount of turn from one line to the other.

Angles are measured in degrees. The symbol for degrees is °.

A right angle is 90 degrees, 90°. A right angle is shown by a small square.

An acute angle is less than 90°.

An obtuse angle is more than 90°.

A straight line has an angle of 180°. This can be used to work out the second angle.

See also protractor

area

Area is the amount of surface of a shape. It is measured in square centimetres. This can be abbreviated to cm^2.

You can work out the **area** of a rectangle by multiplying the length of the shape by the breadth. Length × breadth = **area**.

ascending

From smallest to largest: **ascending** order.
5   69   235   954   1384

See also descending

axis, axes

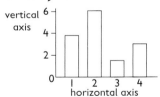

Graphs and charts have two **axes**.

The horizontal **axis** shows the range of data.
The vertical **axis** shows the frequency. They can be labelled in any equal divisions.

See also data

brackets

Brackets are used in maths for grouping parts of calculations together.
10 − (3 + 4) = 7
(10 − 3) + 4 = 11

The calculations in brackets need to be worked out first.

capacity

Capacity is the *amount* that something will hold.
Capacity is measured in litres and millilitres.
1 litre is equal to 1000 millilitres.

Litre can be abbreviated to l.
Millilitres can be abbreviated to ml.

Capacity can also be measured in pints and gallons.

See imperial units

column addition

When you add large numbers, using the standard vertical method can make the calculation easier.

The numbers must be written with the digits of the same place value underneath each other.

If the digits in one column add up to more than 9, the tens are carried to the next column.

Th	H	T	U
6	9	2	5
+ 2	6	4	8
9	5	7	3
1		1	

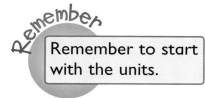

Remember to start with the units.

Hth	Th	H	T	U
2	9	6	8	3
	4	9	7	5
+ 1	6	2	1	3
5	0	8	7	1
2	1	1	1	

◄ You can use this method for more than two numbers.

If you use this method with decimal numbers then the decimal points must be underneath one another.

column subtraction

When you subtract large numbers, using the standard vertical method can make the calculation easier. The numbers must be written with the digits of the same place value underneath each other.

Th	H	T	U
4 5	17	1 2	5
− 3	8	0	6
1	9	1	9

◄ If the top digit is lower than the bottom digit then 10 can be "borrowed" from the next column.

If you use this method with decimal numbers, then the decimal points must be underneath one another.

consecutive

A **consecutive** number is the *next* number.
The **consecutive** number for 5 is 6.

co-ordinates

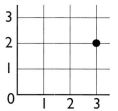

Co-ordinates are numbers or letters that help us to plot the exact position of something. We use them on maps, graphs or charts.

◄ Graphs like this are called the first quadrant.
On the graph, the dot is at (3, 2) 3 lines across and 2 lines up.
To read **co-ordinates** we look *across* and *up*. Some people remember this by thinking of "Along the corridor, up the stairs".

data

Data is information. Interpreting **data** means working out what information is telling you.

A database is a way of storing data. An address book is a data base. A chart is a data base.

decimals

Decimal fractions show us the part of a number that is not a whole number.

H	T	U	•	ths	hdths
		5	•	8	
		5	•	8	6

The decimal point separates the whole numbers from the decimal fractions.

◀ Each digit after the decimal point has a different place value.

5·8 is a number with one decimal place.
5·86 is a number with two decimal places.

Ordering decimals

We **order** decimal numbers by comparing the digits, starting from the left, as this is the highest value digit. If these two digits are the same then we compare the next two digits, and so on.

41·8⑤ — These 3 digits are the same.
41·8⑨ — We compare these 2 digits to order these numbers.

Rounding decimals

To round a decimal to the to the nearest whole number, we look at the tenths digit. If the digit is 5 or more, we round the number *up* to the next whole number. If the digit is less than 5, we round the number *down* to the next whole number.

8.**26** will be rounded down to 8 to make 8.**1**
8.**59** will be rounded up to 9 to make 8.**7**

Decimals and fractions

All decimals have a fraction equivalent. To find the decimal equivalent for a fraction we divide 1 by the denominator and then multiply by the numerator.

$\frac{3}{4} = 0·75$
$1 ÷ 4 = 0·25$
$0·25 × 3 = 0·75$

$\frac{1}{2} = 0·5$
$\frac{1}{4} = 0·25$
$\frac{3}{4} = 0·75$
$\frac{1}{10} = 0·1$
$\frac{3}{10} = 0·3$
$\frac{1}{5} = 0·2$
$\frac{1}{100} = 0·01$
$\frac{3}{100} = 0·003$

See *also* fractions

descending

From largest to smallest: **descending** order.
1384   954   235   69   5

See *also* ascending

difference   When finding the **difference** between numbers, we find how many *more* or *less* one number is than another.

digit   Numbers are made up of **digits**.

        5 is a single-or one-digit number
      23 is a two-digit number
    147 is a three-digit number
   2082 is a four-digit number
  63 581 is a five-digit number
987 206 is a six-digit number

Each **digit** in a number represents a different value.

See also place value

divisibility   There are some quick tests you can do to see if one number will divide by another.

You can use your knowledge of multiplication facts: $3 \times 4 = 12$ so 12 is divisible by 3 and 4.

Other tests:

2s   Any even number is divisible by 2.

4s   If you can divide the last two digits of the number by 4 exactly, the whole number will divide exactly by 4. 216 is divisible by 4 as 16 is divisible by 4.

5s   You can divide 5 exactly into any number ending in 5 or 0.

10s   If a number ends in 0 you can divided it by 10 exactly.

100s   If a number ends in two zeros it will divide exactly by 100.

dividing by 10 and 100   When a number is **divided by 10** the digits move one place value to the right. If the units digit is zero it disappears, if it is not zero it becomes a decimal tenth.

The place value of the digits decrease 10 times.

When a number is **divided by 100** the digits move two place values to the right. If the tens and units digits are zero they disappear, if not they become decimals, hundredths and tenths.

The place value of the digits decreases 100 times.

See also multiplying by 10 and 100

division facts   **Division facts** are the all the division calculations that correspond to the multiplication facts.

$4 \times 5 = 20$
$20 \div 5 = 4$

See also multiplication facts

equivalent fractions	**Equivalent fractions** are fractions of equal value. They are worth the same.
	$\frac{4}{8}$ is equivalent to $\frac{1}{2}$
	Equivalent fractions can be worked out by multiplying the numerator and the denominator by the same number.
	$$\frac{1}{2} \times \frac{2}{2} = \frac{2}{4} \times \frac{2}{2} = \frac{4}{8} \times \frac{2}{2} = \frac{8}{16} \times \frac{2}{2} = \frac{16}{32}$$
	Or by dividing the numerator and the denominator by the same number.
	See also fractions
estimate	An **estimate** is a sensible guess.
	1997 + 2109. The answer is approximately 4000.
	See also approximate
factor	A **factor** is a whole number which will divide exactly into another whole number.
	The factors of 12 are 1, 2, 3, 4, 6, 12 as they all divide into 12.
	The factors can be put into pairs. If the pairs are multiplied together they will equal 12.
	1×12
	2×6
	3×4
figures	A whole number can be written in **figures**: 485 or in **words**: four hundred and eighty five
formula	A **formula** is a way of writing down a rule.
	For example, to find the area of a rectangle you multiply the length by the width.
fractions	**Fractions** are parts of something.
	$\frac{1}{2}$ ──► numerator $\phantom{\frac{1}{2}}$ ──► denominator
	The numerator tells you how many parts we are talking about. The denominator tells you how many parts the whole has been split into.
fractions and division	We find fractions of amounts by dividing by the denominator and then multiplying by the numerator.
	We divide by the denominator as this is the number of parts the amount needs to be divided into. We then multiply by the numerator as this is the number of parts we are talking about.
	See also fractions

halving	To **halve** a number you divide it by 2.

halving

To **halve** a number you divide it by 2.
Half 12 = 6
$12 \div 2 = 6$

Doubling and halving are inverse operations.

See also inverse operations

imperial units

These used to be the standard measurements in Britain. They have now been replaced by metric units. Some imperial units are still used today.

Capacity
Pints and gallons
8 pints = 1 gallon

Length
Miles
1 mile = 1·6 km

improper fractions

An **improper fraction** is a fraction where the numerator is more than the denominator.

$\frac{13}{5}$

These are sometimes called top heavy fractions.
Improper fractions can be changed to whole numbers or mixed numbers.

◄ $\frac{5}{4} = 1\frac{1}{4}$

◄ $\frac{8}{4} = 2$

A fraction that is not an **improper fraction** is a proper fraction.

See also fractions
See also mixed numbers

integer

Integer is another name for a whole number.

See also whole number

inverse operations

Inverse means *the opposite operation*. The **inverse operation** will undo the first operation.

Addition and subtraction are **inverse operations**:
17 + 26 = 43   43 − 26 = 17

Multiplication and division are **inverse operations**:
6 × 9 = 54   54 ÷ 9 = 6

length

Length is how long an object or a distance is.
Length is measured in kilometres, metres, centimetres and millimetres.

1 kilometre is equal to 1000 metres.
1 metre is equal to 100 centimetres.
1 centimetre is equal to 10 millimetres.

Kilometre can be abbreviated to km.
Metre can be abbreviated to m.
Centimetre can be abbreviated to cm.
Millimetre can be abbreviated to mm.

Length can also be measured in miles.

See also imperial units

long multiplication

```
    3 5 2
×     2 7
  7 0 4 0
  2 4 6 4
  9 5 0 4
      1
```

When you multiply numbers which are too large to work out mentally, you can use **long multiplication**. We call it **long multiplication** when both numbers involved are more than a single-digit.

The numbers must be written with the digits of the same place value underneath each other.

See also short multiplication

mass

Mass is another word for weight.
Mass is measured in grams and kilograms.
1 kilogram is equal to 1000 grams.

mixed number

A **mixed number** is a number that has a whole number and a fraction.

$2\frac{1}{4}$ $5\frac{1}{2}$ $7\frac{3}{8}$

See also fractions

mode

The **mode** of a set of data is the number that occurs most often.

multiplication

Multiplication is the inverse operation to division.
Numbers can be multiplied in any order and the answer will be the same.
$5 \times 9 = 45$ $9 \times 5 = 45$

See also inverse operations

multiplying by 10 and 100

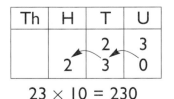

$23 \times 10 = 230$

Our number system is based around 10.
When a number is **multiplied by 10** the digits move one place value to the left and zero goes in the empty column to keep its place value.

◀ The place value of the digits increases 10 times.

When a number is **multiplied by 100** the digits move two place values to the left and zeros go in the empty columns to keep their place value.

The place value of the digits increases 100 times.

See also dividing by 10 and 100

multiplication facts to 10×10

Multiplication facts are the multiplication calculations from all the tables to 10.

See also division facts

multiples

A **multiple** is a number that can be divided into another number.

2, 4, 6, 8, 10, 12 are all **multiples** of 2 as we can divide 2 into them all.

10, 20, 30, 40, 50, 60, 70 are all **multiples** of 10 as we can divide 10 into them all.

Multiples can be recognised by using the multiplication facts.

See also multiplication facts

negative numbers

Numbers and integers can be positive or **negative**.

Negative integers or numbers are *below* zero.

Negative numbers have a minus sign before them.
−56

Negative numbers are ordered in the same way as positive numbers except they run from right to left.

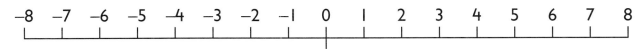

See also positive numbers

net

A **net** is a flat shape which can be cut out and folded up to make a solid shape.

<, >, <, >

are symbols used to order numbers.

< means less than   45<73
> means more than   73>45
< means less than or equal to   45<45, 44
> means more than or equal to 87>87, 88

ordering fractions

When you **order fractions** and mixed numbers, first look at the whole numbers then the fractions. If the fractions have different denominators, think about the fractions in relation to a half to help you to order them.

ordinal

Ordinal numbers show the place of ordered items.

First, second, third, fourth, fifth, sixth, seventh, eighth, ninth, tenth …
1st, 2nd, 3rd, 4th, 5th, 6th, 7th, 8th, 9th, 10th …

parallel

Parallel lines are lines that are the same distance apart all the way along.

◀ They are often shown by two little arrows.

percentage

The sign % stands for per cent, which means out of 100. 30% means 30 out of 100.

Percentages are linked to fractions and decimals.

$\frac{1}{2}$ = 50% = 0·5

$\frac{1}{4}$ = 25% = 0·25

$\frac{3}{4}$ = 75% = 0·75

$\frac{1}{5}$ = 20% = 0·2

$\frac{1}{10}$ = 10% = 0·10

Finding percentages of amounts

To find **percentages** of amounts we need to use the relationship to fractions.

To find 50% of an amount, we divide by 2: 50% = $\frac{1}{2}$. 50% of £40 is £20.

To find 25% we divide by 4: 25% = $\frac{1}{4}$
To find 20% we divide by 5: 20% = $\frac{1}{5}$

perpendicular

A **perpendicular** line meets another line at right angles.

perimeter

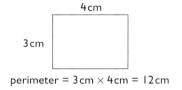

4cm

3cm

perimeter = 3cm × 4cm = 12cm

Perimeter is the distance all the way around a flat shape.

You can calculate the **perimeter** of a shape by adding the length of all the sides together.

If a shape has sides all the same length then you can use multiplication to work out the **perimeter**.

place value

The **place value** of a digit is what it is *worth*.

In **467** the **place value** of the 6 is 60 or 6 tens.
In **624** the **place value** of the 6 is 600 or 6 hundreds.

See also digit

positive numbers

Numbers and integers can be **positive** or negative.

Positive numbers or integers are above zero. They can be written with a + sign before them. If there is no sign before a number it is always counted as positive.

See also negative numbers

probability

Probability is about how *likely* or *unlikely* the outcome of an event is. The event maybe the throw of a die or whether or not it will rain today.

We use certain words to discuss **probability**. We can put events and the words on a scale from *no chance of it happening* to *certain*.

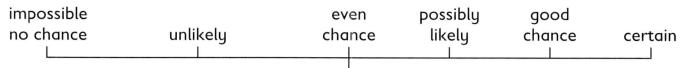

impossible no chance | unlikely | even chance | possibly likely | good chance | certain

Even chance means an event is as likely to happen as not happen.

product

Product is another name for the answer to a multiplication calculation.

24 is the product of 6×4

proportion

Proportion shows the relationship between two connected things.

When amounts are being compared and they have equal ratios they are in **proportion**.

1 packet of biscuits costs 60p
2 packets of biscuits cost £1·20
3 packets cost £1·80
The cost is in **proportion** to the number of packets bought.

See also ratio

protractor

A **protractor** is used to draw and measure angles. **Protractors** can be circular or semi-circular.

quotient

Quotient is another name for the answer to a division calculation.

The remainder of the **quotient** can be shown as a fraction or a decimal fraction.

$27 \div 4 = 6 \text{ r } 3$
$27 \div 4 = 6\frac{3}{4}$
$27 \div 4 = 6·75$

As we are dividing by 4, the fraction will be a quarter and there are 3 of them left. 0·75 is the decimal equivalent to $\frac{3}{4}$.

range

The **range** of a set of data is the lowest to the highest value.

ratio

Ratio is a way of comparing amounts or numbers.

It can be used in two ways:

It can describe the relationship between *part to whole*.
A cake is divided into 4 equal parts and one part is eaten. The **ratio** of part to whole is one part in every four parts or 1 in 4.

Or it can describe the relationship of *part to other part*.
A cake is divided into 4 parts and one part is eaten. The ratio of part to part is 1 to 3 as for every piece eaten three pieces are left.

The **ratio** 1 to 3 can also be written as 1:3.

See also proportion

reflection

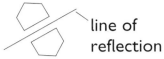
line of reflection

◀ If a shape is **reflected**, it is drawn as it would appear reflected in a mirror held against or alongside one of its sides.

reflective symmetry

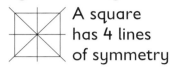
A square has 4 lines of symmetry

A shape is symmetrical if both sides are the same when a line is drawn through the shape. The line can be called a mirror line or an axes.

◀ Some shapes have more than one line of symmetry.

rounding

To **round** a number *to the nearest* 10, we look at the units digit.

If it is 5 or greater, we round the it up to the next 10. **345** rounds up to 350

If it is less than 5, we round it down to the previous 10. **343** rounds down to 340

To **round** a number *to the nearest* 100, we look at the tens digit.

If it is 5 or greater, we round it up to the next 100. **462** rounds up to 500

If it is less than 5, we round it down to the previous 100. **437** rounds down to 400

To **round** a number to the nearest 1000, we look at the hundreds digit.

If it is 5 or greater, we round it up to the next 1000. **2768** rounds up to 3000

If it is less than 5, we round it down to the previous 1000. **2469** rounds down to 2000

scales

Scales are used on measuring equipment. Not all divisions are labelled, so to read a scale accurately you need to work out what each division represents. This varies from scale to scale.

short division

When you divide numbers that are too large to work out mentally, you can use **short division**. We call it **short division** when one of the numbers involved is a single-digit.

short multiplication

When you multiply numbers that are too large to work mentally, you can use **short multiplication**. We call it **short multiplication** when one of the numbers involved is a single-digit.

	3	4	6
×			9
3	1	1	4
		4	5

◀ The numbers must be written with the digits of the same place value underneath each other.

See also long multiplication

square numbers

To **square** a number it is multiplied by itself. The answer is a **square number**.

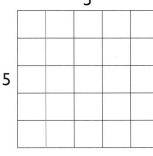

5

5

To square 5, we multiply 5 by itself. 25 is the **square number**.

◀ 5 × 5 = 25 can also be written as $5^2 = 25$

Square numbers have an odd number of factors. The factors of 25 are 1, 5, 25.

Square numbers up to 100

1 × 1 = **1**
2 × 2 = **4**
3 × 3 = **9**
4 × 4 = **16**
5 × 5 = **25**
6 × 6 = **36**
7 × 7 = **49**
8 × 8 = **64**
9 × 9 = **81**
10 × 10 = **100**

See *also* factor

symmetrical pattern

Patterns can be **symmetrical**. They may have two lines of symmetry.

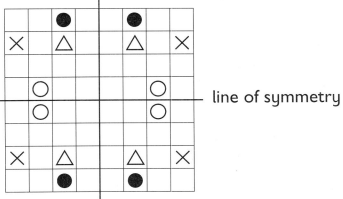

line of symmetry

line of symmetry

time

These are the units **time** is measured in:
seconds
minutes
hours
days
weeks
months
years

These are the relationships between these units:
60 seconds = 1 minute
60 minutes = 1 hour
24 hours = 1 day
7 days = 1 week
4 weeks = 1 month
12 months = 1 year
365 days = 1 year

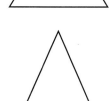

analogue clock   digital clock

Time can be read on analogue clocks or digital clocks.

Digital clocks can be 12 hour or 24 hour.
The 12-hour clock uses a.m. and p.m.
The 24-hour clock carries on after 12 o'clock midday to 24 instead of starting at 1 again.

translation

A **translation** is when a shape is moved by sliding it.

triangles

A **triangle** is a 2D shape with three straight sides and three angles.

There are four kinds of triangle:

Equilateral triangle
This has three equal sides and three equal angles.

Isosceles triangle
This has two equal sides. The angles opposite these two sides are also equal.

Scalene triangle

All three sides are different lengths.
The angles are all different too.

Right-angled triangle
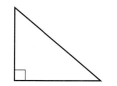
This has one right angle.

whole number

A **whole number** is a number without decimals or fractions.
See also integer